What I Learned from *Mom*

27 Celebrated Individuals on How Mother's Wisdom Shaped Their Lives

JEFFREY D. DUNN

AND

SHERRIE ROLLINS WESTIN

A REGALO PRESS BOOK
ISBN: 979-8-88845-186-1
ISBN (eBook): 979-8-88845-187-8

What I Learned from Mom:
27 Celebrated Individuals on How Mother's Wisdom Shaped Their Lives
© 2026 by Jeffrey D. Dunn and Sherrie Rollins Westin
All Rights Reserved

Cover Design by Jim Villaflores

Publishing Team:
Founder and Publisher – Gretchen Young
Editorial Assistant – Caitlyn Limbaugh
Managing Editor – Caitlin Burdette
Production Manager – Kate Harris
Production Editor – Rachel Paul

As part of the mission of Regalo Press, a donation is being made to Sesame Workshop, as chosen by the author. Find out more about this organization at https://sesameworkshop.org/.

Regalo Press
New York • Nashville
regalopress.com

Published in the United States of America
2 3 4 5 6 7 8 9 10

For Joan Ganz Cooney

The Mother of Sesame Street

CONTENTS

HOW THIS BOOK BEGAN

Jeffrey D. Dunn

Photo Credit: Jeffrey D. Dunn

"*I* am, very proudly my mother's son."
That is how I concluded the eulogy to my mother,
Sylvia Guild Dunn, after she passed away on Halloween

night in 2015. Long before, I had realized full well that I was mostly the man that she had made. As I wrote my remarks, I knew that I wanted to try to give back some of what she had given to me, and the seedling idea for this book was born.

My mother was one of the most organized people I have ever known. She was smart, and she was ambitious. She was also a motivator. For the longest time, she exercised her talents leading various women's groups, from the garden club to the volunteer corps at a local hospital. These were the traditional paths that were open to women of her generation and background. If she had been born in a later generation, I have no doubt that she would have been the leader of a company. She was, quite simply, a woman who lived before her time.

When I was twelve years old, we moved to a larger house, and all three children finally got their own bedroom. For mine, Mom framed and hung on my walls sayings that were important to her and that she wanted me to take to heart.

The first was a part of a poem she hung above my headboard, where I saw it each night when I climbed into bed:

> *One ship sails East,*
> *And another West,*
> *By the same self-winds that blow,*
> *'Tis the set of their sails*
> *And not the gales*
> *That tells the way that we go.*

She hung another New England adage on the wall to the side of my bed, where I would see it each morning when I got up:

Use it up, Wear it out, Make it do, Or do without.

Finally, on the wall next to my student desk, she hung a framed lithograph depicting the famed minuteman statue at the Old North Bridge in Concord, Massachusetts. Inscribed on its base is a part of the Ralph Waldo Emerson poem that commemorated the Battles of Lexington and Concord and the start of the American Revolution, which my early ancestors fought in:

By the rude bridge that arched the flood,
Their flags to April's breeze unfurled,
Here once the embattled farmers stood
And fired the shot heard 'round the world.

The wisdom she wanted me to absorb from all of this could be summed up like this:

- You are responsible for your own success in life; don't blame others or circumstances.
- Don't be wasteful. Be careful with your resources, because there will always be future financial challenges to navigate, and a disposable world isn't good for people or the planet.
- Everyone can make a difference. However, you must also be willing to do the right thing and stand up and be counted when the times demand it. The most honorable and courageous people are the ones

who stand up for what is right, especially when others do not and when the personal cost of doing so may be very high.

My mother saw to it that the bedroom in which I grew up served as a daily prompting of how she expected me to go forth and live my life. Those aphorisms became deeply rooted in my brain and, over time, helped to propel me from my childhood bedroom all the way to the boardrooms of Boston, New York, and London. I eventually chose to become the first outsider to lead Sesame Workshop, the remarkable nonprofit educational organization behind *Sesame Street,* in large part because its mission and work to help children everywhere grow smarter, stronger, and kinder aligned so well with those values and ideals that my mother espoused and instilled in me.

I also felt that I probably wasn't alone in the lessons that I had received, which is what has inspired this book. I knew how well my mother had prepared and guided me and that others had likely similarly been deeply influenced by their mothers' teachings. I thought that if we could capture a broad range of these lessons and inspirations, it would throw a well-deserved spotlight on the importance of mothers in shaping the character of our society.

This book, then, is all about moms and some of the remarkable men and women that they eventually made. It showcases the lessons that they gifted to their children, which stuck with them and guided them into adulthood and accomplishment in their chosen field.

Sherrie Rollins Westin

Photo Credit: Sherrie Rollins Westin

As we began interviewing people for this book, we heard so many compelling stories about people's mothers—the lives they led and the examples they set. As a listener, you could hear the clear through lines from their mothers to the successful people they became. For me, working on this book constantly made me think of the expression "The apple doesn't fall far from the tree."

The more I thought about it, the more I could see that the same could be said for me, even literally. I grew up in the middle of an apple orchard in Roanoke, Virginia, and apples loomed large in many of our family traditions. I have so many fond memories of time spent in the top of those apple trees, with rope ladders and tree forts—and more often than not, my mother was right alongside us! It epitomized my mom's playful spirit. She kept climbing those apple trees until she was eighty-two years old and only stopped because she fractured her hip when she was in the top of a tree and the branch broke. When I asked her why on earth she was *still* climbing trees in her eighties, she said she was just stringing up Christmas lights, and they look so much nicer when they go up high.

My mother, Charlotte Weeks Sandy, was in her early twenties, just a year after she married my dad, when she had me. She *loved* motherhood and always had so much fun being a mom. In a sense, my little brothers and I were like her playmates. She loved games and sports and was fiercely competitive. She made sure we learned how to horseback ride, play tennis, water and snow ski, and sail. And, if it was a sport she hadn't yet taken up, she was right there with us taking lessons.

Mom was always coming up with clever ideas for projects and parties. For example, when we bought a new refrigerator, Mom not only turned the huge box it came in into a puppet theater, but she also made us marionettes so we could stage puppet shows for ourselves and our friends.

In addition to her love of children, Mom loves animals. If an animal was hurt or in need of rescue, the neighborhood kids brought it to Mom. When I was in fourth grade, our yellow lab, Sandy, had thirteen puppies. We were so excited and named each one. Early on, Sandy got an infection, and she could not nurse for several days. The vet told us that the puppies were not going to make it. Mom would have none of it! I remember staying up all night with her as she forced Karo syrup from a medicine dropper into their little mouths, one by one. I helped by keeping track and rotating all thirteen of them throughout the night. And they all made it!

That is my mom. She is so determined, and she never gives up on anyone or anything.

So how far from the tree did this apple fall? I had never given it much thought before this book, because in some obvious ways, our lives are very different. I have worked since right out of college. I did not have children until my late thirties and early forties. And I live outside New York City—a far cry from Roanoke.

But in many other ways, I can clearly see that I am my mother's daughter. I like to think I brought much of Mom's same playful spirit in raising my own two children, Lily and David Palmer. I've worked hard to create family and neighborhood traditions, so they will look back on their childhoods with the kind of fond memories I am so fortunate to have. I know I have my mother's hard work ethic and determination, and for that I am grateful. These are traits my mother has in spades.

For the past twenty-seven years, I've also been part of another family—the much larger family that is Sesame Workshop, the nonprofit educational organization that produces *Sesame Street* around the world and helps children everywhere grow smarter, stronger, and kinder. We base our work on research that helps put children on the best path to succeed in school and life. So much of what I've learned is what my mother intuitively knew: that childhood play is essential to a child's healthy development and *the most* important way for a child to learn is through engagement with a caring adult.

But as every mother knows, not all of caring for those entrusted to our care is joyful play. There are anxious moments when we are called on to do all in our power to protect and defend. I had one of those times in the fall of 2021, when members of the Sesame extended family in Afghanistan were in harm's way. For more than ten years, we produced a local version of *Sesame Street* in Afghanistan, which focused on gender equity and girls' education, funded by the U.S. Department of State. When the U.S. pulled its troops out of Afghanistan (and many of our Afghan colleagues were in danger, targeted by the Taliban, and desperate to leave), I began working night and day to try to help evacuate as many as possible. I don't think I have ever worked as hard or been as determined to try to do what seemed, at times, impossible. In the end, we were able to help fifty escape, and they are now in the process of resettlement in the U.S. and Canada. During the most harrowing and discouraging moments of this daunting task, when we were told again and again that it could not work, I found myself thinking of my mom. Giving up was not an option.

I would like to think that this apple didn't fall that far from my mom's tree after all. I am hugely grateful to her for being the role model she has been as a mother and grandmother. I know we share many traits and values, but there's one big difference between us: When I'm eighty-two, I will definitely have someone else string up my outdoor Christmas lights!

Photo Credit: Tory Burch

NEGATIVITY IS NOISE

Tory Burch

My mother, Reva, is my perennial inspiration. It is impossible to sum up what she means to me in a few paragraphs, but I will give it a try.

So much of what I learned from her about ambition, independence, style, and strength started with her mother, Lillian.

Lillian was extraordinary and ahead of her time: a concert violinist who played a Stradivarius and became one of the first women orchestra leaders in the United States in the 1920s and '30s. She was also an incredible mom, a fantastic cook, and someone who always gave back. My grandmother showed her daughter—and me—that you can carve your own path, live on your own terms, and never allow anyone to put you in a box.

She raised my mother to be adventurous and independent. My mom went to Emerson College in the '50s, moved to Greenwich Village, and worked as a model and actress. We grew up hearing stories about her friends and "dates," including everyone from Steve McQueen (before he was

Steve McQueen) to Marlon Brando. In her early twenties, she met my father and knew right away that he was the one.

Buddy Robinson was reserved with a wicked sense of humor. He was a man of few words, but when he spoke, everyone listened. He was known to be the ultimate dandy and had an innate sense of style; he designed all his own clothing, lining his dinner jackets with Hermès scarves and wearing Gucci loafers before they were the chic thing to wear.

My father was the quintessential "bachelor" and had books of the beautiful women he dated, including Grace Kelly. He was forty-three when he met my mother; it was love at first sight. He fell madly in love and knew he finally wanted to get married. And once my parents were together, they were never apart; as my mother put it, they were "crazy for each other" every day for fifty years.

One of the decisions they made as a young couple was to raise our family on a "gentleman's farm" in Valley Forge, Pennsylvania. We moved there in the middle of a snowstorm, when I was a baby. Their idea was to create an oasis away from society—complete with a menagerie of horses, ducks, German shepherds, and cats—and live in a more grounded way, surrounded by nature and family. My brother Jamie described our childhood as "Huck Finn meets Andy Warhol." Our parents wanted us to have a different kind of childhood—to appreciate all the small miracles of being a kid, whether it was making dandelion wine, drinking hot chocolate after a day of sledding, or climbing trees and collecting rocks. We rarely watched TV, and we learned how to entertain ourselves.

They taught us to embrace differences in people and to be open to new ideas. To surround ourselves with beauty and to always be intellectually curious. Every dinner was centered around our family: storytelling, beautiful flowers, and tables always decorated by my mother.

People are often surprised to hear I was a complete tomboy back then. Growing up with three brothers, we lived outside—and so did our mom, working in her organic garden for eight hours a day. My brothers and I would only be expected to come home when the dinner bell rang at 6:00 p.m.

Growing up, my parents taught us to dream big. My mother encouraged me to be ambitious, and from a very young age, she taught me how to believe in myself. Whenever I experienced self-doubt, she would say, "You're Tory Robinson. You can do anything!"

Years later, when I started working on my company, she continued to support me unconditionally. My mother told me that I needed to thicken my skin; she knew people would have much to say and that starting a company wouldn't be easy. She always reminded me to ignore the naysayers, to look forward, and to follow my instincts.

To my mom, the glass is always half full, and when things got tough, she reminded us that tomorrow is a new day. She always had a lot of advice (and still does), but one of the most important things she would say is that "negativity is noise." She lived her life by these words and taught me and my brothers to live by them, as well.

She raised the four of us equally, and it never occurred to me that I might be treated differently than my brothers because I was a girl. She knew that women faced unique challenges, and in her way she was preparing me for the future. My mom was always telling us stories about women in history at the dinner table, and she spoke about "women's liberation," as she called it then. I have vivid memories of my mom telling me about the day she finally got a credit card in her name; she was angry that it took until 1974.

She was an entrepreneur; when I was in high school, she started a flower business and put my brothers and me to work. We saw how gratifying it was to work hard and see extraordinary results.

Every summer, my parents took six-week vacations to Greece, Italy, Morocco, India, and beyond. They met new friends and collected beautiful things along the way, and their wanderlust most definitely rubbed off on me. The unique world they created on our farm was the original inspiration for my company. Photos of their trips were all over my early moodboards, and their style made a lasting impression. They dressed similarly to how they decorated our home: with color and eclecticism. Everything was chic and lived-in, never too perfect or overdone.

Their style translated to how they lived their lives and how they treated others. My mother used to tell me that I had to treat everyone the same, whether it was the queen of England or the cabdriver. She used to say, "You never learn anything with your mouth open," and she told my brothers that being a gentleman is not a part-time job.

My parents always gave back, and I wanted to do the same since I was a little girl. On the farm, my mom opened our home to an array of people: friends, family, artists, musicians, or anyone who needed a little help. She has incredible compassion and empathy, two things that she instilled in me. I knew that if I ever started a company, my goal would be to create a foundation so I could help others, which I did in 2009 when we established the Tory Burch Foundation.

So thank you, Mom: You are divine and sublime. Thank you for always believing in me and my dreams, and for being the best mom I could have ever hoped to have.

Photo Credit: Ken Burns

SIXTY-ONE YEARS IS TOO LONG TO BE WITHOUT A MOTHER

Ken Burns

My mother, Lyla Smith Tupper, after years and years of illness, died of cancer on April 28, 1965, in Ann Arbor, Michigan, when I was just eleven years old.

At that age, grief is so difficult to understand and process. Our family's situation was compounded by the fact that my father had some kind of undiagnosed mental illness. After the funeral, he never even collected her ashes. Grief has a half-life that is endless, and a large part of my life has been trying to understand the pain I "conveniently" didn't deal with when I was young.

Many years later, when I was approaching forty, I had a conversation with my late father-in-law, an eminent psychologist, and told him that I seemed to be trying to keep my mother alive. I said that all my life, the day of her death, April 28, was always approaching and then receding. I was never present on the actual anniversary.

He said to me, "I bet you blow out the candles on your birthday cake and wish for her to come back." Then, he referred to five or six other intimate things that only I knew

I had done to "keep her alive." How did he know that I asked? He paused and said, "Look at what you do for a living. You wake the dead. You make Abraham Lincoln and Jackie Robinson and Louis Armstrong come alive. Who do you think you are really trying to wake up?"

And so, at that moment, I began a journey with my younger brother, Ric, to come to terms with her death, to find her ashes—to come to terms with all that had been suppressed and forgotten.

A couple of years after that fateful conversation with my father-in-law, I participated in a sociological study about the early death of a parent. Two sociologists came to interview me, and after a few hours, I realized that it was going to take a lot longer than I anticipated. They sensed my unease and finally said, "Okay. One more question. What was your mother's greatest gift to you?"

Instantly, I replied, "Dying."

Then, I started to cry. Of course, I did not want her to die. But I also understood, in that instance, that everything I am today is built on the fact that she *did* die and that I have somehow transformed that loss into something positive: telling the history of my country by "waking the dead."

When I was growing up in Delaware, where our family lived before moving to Michigan, my mother was a force on the block, a resource for our neighbors, even as she was dealing with her terminal illness. It had all begun with a diagnosis of breast cancer, then a radical mastectomy. After a few years, her cancer had metastasized, with horrific consequences for her and her family—us. Yet she maintained a remarkable and heroic cheerfulness. She'd get to the top of a flight of stairs and pull out a flask of whiskey and take a sip to pause and to catch her breath. For a while, she was operating on one lung, then half a lung. She possessed exceptional courage.

I remember once, as a boy of eight or nine, that my mother was so weak she could not get out of bed. We moved a hospital bed into our living room, and she held forth from there. I remember rubbing her feet when they hurt, and I'd sometimes do it for hours.

But whenever my class had a school trip, just as we were getting on the bus, I would get anxious and bail. I understood many years later that I simply didn't want to leave my mother alone. I didn't want to enjoy a simple field trip. I wanted to protect her in some way, but, really, she had been protecting me and my brother.

She was incredibly loving but also expected much from us. She told us to assume responsibility for ourselves and our actions, one of the many lessons that was constantly imparted by her in the midst of a life that was slowly being taken from her.

A few years after she died, I went back to Delaware and met a woman who had shared a hospital room with my mother. "I knew I was getting out, and your mother knew her illness was terminal," she told me. "Yet, she was cheerful and happy and kept my spirits up the whole time I was there. I still feel remorse that I was not able to do much for her. My admiration for her has not lessened over time.

I want you to never forget what an extraordinary woman she was."

She was not the only person who has told me how amazing and strong my mother was. I've heard it a lot over the years. People always want me to know that.

My mother received her death sentence while she was in her thirties. We boys knew something was wrong, but we didn't really find out until I was seven years old and my parents told us she had only six months to live. But my mother pulled me aside and said, "I'll see you to junior high school. Don't worry. Six months is just what the doctors say."

Junior high seemed impossibly far away. In the end, she missed it by just a few months. She stayed alive through a combination of internal strength, willpower, and love for my brother and me. We learned lifelong lessons about strength, fortitude, and generosity from our mother.

I'm seventy-two now. She died when she was forty-two. It seems like forever ago. My brother and I still call her "Mommy." In our minds, she still towers over us in size. I grew to taller than my father, and he had gone from being "Daddy" to "Dad." But she stayed Mommy to us.

When my father passed away, it was a completely different kind of experience. I miss him but not in the same all-encompassing ways I still miss my mother. I've read the many letters my mom wrote to my dad's mom, her mother-in-law. They are filled with compassion, tolerance, forbearance, and, of course, courage. While she was battling her own illness, she thought of me and my brother and our future without her. My father had, as I said, untreated mental issues, and my mother wrote about her anxieties to his mother. "What will happen to my boys when I die? Who will care for them? Bobby (my father) is not going to be able to do it."

When she did die, we muddled through, in part because her strength and fortitude had instilled in us something lasting and imperishable.

All through her seemingly endless sickness, I knew something was desperately wrong. She was hospitalized for long periods of time. My grandmother would come from Baltimore and take care of us. My father was often absent. It was difficult having this deadly sword of Damocles hanging over our lives all the time, and it made my childhood a living hell. My mother's optimism could not mask the reality of what was happening. There was no question I was loved, but the terror was that I would soon lose that love.

When our father told us she had died, my brother cried, and I didn't. I didn't cry until I was nearly forty. It was my own personal crisis—going through a divorce—that made me realize how much her death had imprisoned me. That's what I was talking to my father-in-law about, trying to figure it all out and manage yet another moment of abandonment—now in my adulthood.

Anna Karenina, by Leo Tolstoy, begins with the idea that happy families are all alike, and unhappy families are unhappy in their own ways. We accept that grief, or any other kind of unhappiness, is expressed and understood and internalized in so many different ways and that we just have to tolerate the varieties of negative human experience.

But I've come to think that maybe Tolstoy, whom I greatly admire, got it wrong. My revelation comes from my mother's positive outlook. Maybe *unhappy* families are all the same. I think there is great variety in how we experience joy and that we don't appreciate the dimensions of that joy enough. I still think of my mother as a joyous person despite what she endured, and that, to me, is a remarkable accomplishment.

There is a wonderful coda to Lyla's life. We, of course, didn't call her by her first name. We never said Lyla. She was always Mommy. We knew her name was Lyla, and we'd hear it once in a while from a relative, but after her death, her name was always draped in a kind of metaphoric black crepe until January 18, 2011, when my oldest daughter, Sarah, had a girl that she named Lyla, after a grandmother she never met. From that moment on, the black crepe disappeared. Now, when we say Lyla, birds sing, the flowers bloom. My daughter had given me—given all of us—an amazing gift.

My granddaughter Lyla and my youngest daughter, Willa, are the same age, though my daughter arrived first. They attend the same school, and they are best friends. There is no "aunt" or "niece" spoken or invoked. After almost never hearing it, the name "Lyla" is heard daily. And so, she lives.

My mother also lives in the example I have tried to set and tried to impart to my four daughters, two of whom are the spitting image of my mom. Sarah and my third daughter, Olivia, look exactly like the grandmother they of course never knew. We have their portraits next to each other in our kitchen.

My father was an anthropologist, and I spent the first year of my life in the highest village in the Alps that is occupied year-round. I also have a picture from there of my mother feeding me in a highchair in this little kitchen on a bright, sunny day. That's another metaphor for her. She fed everyone and everything.

She fed me; she fed my brother. She filled us with a kind of purpose and determination to escape the specific gravity of what happened to our family when she died. But I have not made that escape completely. Not a day goes by that I don't think about her and feel that acute sense of loss. She's been gone so long. Sixty-one years is too long to be without a mother.

But we *have* gotten by. We've figured out how to make lemonade out of the lemons given to us by her illness and passing. It is comforting to embrace the paradox that her greatest gift to me is that by her death, she set me on a course to "wake the dead," as my father-in-law observed. I am drawn to sharing these stories that bring us together. The Latin motto of the United States is "E Pluribus Unum," or "out of many, one." We're in danger of rejecting that notion of not only Pluribus but of Unum itself. In a time when we are so fragmented, it is good to have stories that reinforce what unites us. And it comes from not just the tragedy of her passing but also the example that her life was.

If I accept that her greatest gift was dying, then it is also true that that loss tempered me in so many ways, such as being a good father and, I hope, a good filmmaker, I also must acknowledge that her absence still represents a huge deficit in my life. In a funny way, with that constant pain, she *is* alive.

She died on April 28, 1965, and often at 4:28 in the afternoon I would say out loud "Mommy." It's one way I keep her alive.

For many years, I would go back to her grave (when we finally found her ashes), where we had been able to place a plaque with her name and dates. I brought my oldest daughters, Sarah and Lilly; I taught them how to drive there at the cemetery. I'd also tell stories about her, and she'd come alive again. We'd make it a joyful time—as my mother would have wanted.

Many years later I took my younger daughters there, and we did the same thing. After a while, Olivia and Willa became aware of the significance of 4/28/1965. Now we sometimes text each other at 4:28 p.m. and say "Mommy" or "Mama," because that is what they call their mother. It's an amazing bonding device. They have an emotional connection to a woman they never met.

There is another way this deficit I feel from her death has helped me. I have been fortunate enough to realize that whatever parental inattention I experienced due to her and my father's illnesses, and then her death, I was not going to let my daughters suffer from that.

My daughters know that my most important job is to be their father. Both sets of daughters are products of divorce, so I have had to be vigilant. I hate to say this, but those divorces helped me focus on what matters. As a filmmaker, I could have easily been an absent father. But I have not missed their school plays, pageants, recitals, or games. I try to tailor my travel to when I don't have the girls. The lesson I learned from my mother not being around is that I made a priority of being around. My advice is to let the grief in, transform it, and don't miss the important work—perhaps the greatest job there is—of raising children. This is my mother's greatest gift.

Photo Credit: Anna Cathcart

I CAN ONLY BE A SOLO ARTIST BECAUSE I HAD THE BEST BANDMATE

Anna Cathcart

My mom is the first person I call—when I have a stressful day at work, when I have a life-changing decision to make, and when my dishwasher is making a weird sound—often at 2:00 a.m. Not only does she always pick up, but she never hangs up first.

My mother, Mamie Cathcart, would do anything to help me, at any given time. She's driven an hour to drop off a poster board I forgot for a school project, stayed up late finishing a load of laundry because I need *that* shirt for tomorrow, and patiently listened to me rant about the same thing for the hundredth time. In addition to offering unwavering support with no questions asked, she simply exists on the same wavelength.

In my first year of college, I was being initiated into a club, and one of the challenges was to call our parents and, without context, tell them we were dropping out of school. I immediately volunteered to call my mom because I knew she would not only get the joke but would absolutely love being a part of it. As expected, my mom played along perfectly, making everyone laugh on speakerphone, and texted me right after, saying, "I hope you have the best night ever and I can't wait to hear all about it!" I remember feeling in that moment an overwhelming sense of gratitude for who my mom is.

If you've got good news, you'll want to share it with my mom—because she'll make it feel like the greatest news in the world. Balloons, streamers, cheers, and applause were regular features of my childhood home. My mother has an unparalleled ability to not only notice the little things but celebrate them. The item we were planning to buy at the grocery store is on sale? *Best. Day. Ever.* We found a parking spot right away? *How could it possibly get any better?* Luckily, this joyful attitude has rubbed off on me. (I mean seriously, how can you not get excited when the item you were already planning to buy is suddenly on sale?!) My friends often laugh, saying they've never met anyone as easily excited as my mom. In fact, when my best friend from high school got into her dream college, she drove straight to our house—cake in hand—to share the news with my mom and me. We were the very first people she wanted to tell, because in the Cathcart household, every success—no matter how big or small or who it's for—feels like a monumental victory, all thanks to my mom.

Our front door wasn't just open for good news—it was open for anything. Whether it was the first day of school, the last day of school, a birthday, or even a bad day, my friends were always at our house. I can't count how many times I heard, "I miss your kitchen counter" when they hadn't been over in a while. My mom loved being the keeper of that counter, creating a space where everyone felt loved, seen, and celebrated. I don't think I'll ever be able to fully express how grateful I am for that.

We're a close-knit family of four: my mom, my dad, my older sister, Sara, and me. Sara is my best friend and, frankly, my favorite person in the world—it's always been this way. The two of us have never had a rough patch, never had a fight. I look up to her in every way, and I have no idea who I'd be today if it wasn't for her. Despite my sister and me being partners in crime since birth, it often felt like my mom and I were a power duo throughout my childhood.

For example, let me walk you through a typical Cathcart family ski trip. My dad and sister would be up at 7:00 a.m., ready to tackle black diamond runs all day, while my mom and I would sleep in until 10:30 a.m., enjoy a leisurely breakfast, and slowly—sometimes very slowly—make our way through the local town. This wasn't because we were lazy (at least that's what we'd like to say), but because we simply mastered the art of doing nothing. We'd spend hours chatting, browsing bookstores, looking at knickknacks, and wandering into bakeries, sometimes purely to admire the croissants in the window. We didn't need a destination— the *wander* was always enough for my mom and me.

One of the most defining moments in my relationship with my mom came when I unexpectedly began my acting career. I always wanted to be an actor but never thought it could be more than a dream on my vision board. After completing my very first audition for film/TV, I landed the lead role of Agent Olympia on the PBS/TVOKids series *Odd Squad*. I was only twelve at the time, and I didn't know my world was about to be turned upside down. I found out I booked the role on a Wednesday, and by Saturday, my mom and I were on a plane to Toronto to start shooting.

My mom's support was immeasurable. She packed a suitcase, hopped on a plane, and held my hand as we dove into the unknown. Shortly, it became routine for her to wake me up for every early morning call time, making sure I was ready and prepped for my packed schedule—all with a smile on her face, excited to see what adventure today would bring. We were both continuously learning what it meant to work in this industry, and as I focused on my new role, she took on the role of my biggest cheerleader, my emotional support system, and the eyes I could look for in every room to instantly feel comforted. We didn't know it at the time, but this was the start of what would turn into seven years of working as an actress with my mom by my side.

Those years were incredibly formative for me, both as an actor and as a person. They were also transformative years for my entire family, filled with change, adjustment, and sacrifice. While my mom and I moved to Toronto, my dad and sister stayed behind in Vancouver. It was especially hard on them, particularly my sister, who suddenly had to navigate her senior year of high school without us. Not once did my dad or sister make me feel guilty about causing this whirlwind. Instead, they offered unconditional support, understanding, love, and excitement. I'll never fully be able to express how much that's meant to me. As my career expanded, more flights were booked, more pressures were added, and I was faced with constant changes. The one thing that didn't change? My mom and I were a team.

Now in my early twenties, as I try and navigate my career as an adult, one of the greatest challenges is learning what this "team" might look like. In the last few years, acting has gone from an extracurricular to a full-time career for me. Naturally, with this shift came a shift in my mom's role as well. In a lot of ways, this career had been hers for seven years too. She committed her life to it, spending just as many hours on set as me, learning the ins and outs of the industry, and constantly finding the best ways to support me. Now, something that has always been *ours* is slowly becoming mine. It's almost like we've been a band for years, and now I'm breaking out as a solo artist. Needless to say, this is not easy for the band.

I think my mom can sometimes forget the only reason I'm brave enough to break out as a "solo artist" is because of the skills I learned and the love I've received from my bandmate. My mother was my constant role model, not only showing me how to compose a business email and handle coordinating airport pick-up times, but she's taught me how to move with strength, kindness, confidence, intelligence, and so many other good words. All by simply being herself. I learned how to be *me* because of her. I have no idea where I'd be without my mom, but I know it wouldn't be close to where I am today.

So, as I continue to step out on stage, even as a solo artist, it will always feel like she's right there with me. Maybe it's because I know she'll always be there cheering me on in the front row, proudly watching me shine, wearing a t-shirt with my face on it. Throughout all these changes, I know I can trust at least one constant: She'll always be my biggest fan, and she'll always be the first person I call when I get the perfect parking spot.

Photo Credit: Chelsea Clinton

OUR FAMILY WAS THE CENTER OF HER WORLD

Chelsea Clinton

My earliest memory involves my mom. I fell down the stairs, and I remember her picking me up, hugging me, and then reading *Goodnight, Moon* to me. I was just two and a half years old, but I remember it vividly. We were living in the house on Midland Street in Little Rock, between my father's first and second terms as governor of Arkansas.

I didn't realize until I became a mom myself the impact of such a positive, affirmative memory. For as long as I can remember, I've felt a kind of safety and security, thanks to my mom (and dad).

Despite the hecticness and demands of their professional lives, my parents prioritized quantity *and* quality of time with me. I always felt that I had a lot of time with my parents. That created this belief that I had a secure launching pad for when I went out into the world as a kid, and later as an adult.

My mother was always looking out for me and taught me a lot. We had a swing set in the backyard of the governor's mansion, and one time I was swinging and my fingers got pinched in the chain that the seat is attached to. My mom put ice on it and gave me a lot of cuddles. But she also reminded me that she had told me to watch out for the chain when I was using the swing. It was a painful lesson that reminded me to listen to my mother!

It was clearly important to my mom to be engaged in my life. She went to all my games, ballet recitals, and choir performances. She was in the PTA. When she had to work on the weekends, I went to her office with her, which I also did with my dad. I saw and heard her working while I was coloring or drawing or writing a story. And when she had to travel for a bar association meeting, I went with her.

I loved feeling like a part of her world. I understood her world wasn't just our family, but that our family was the center of her world. I always knew, without question, that I was the most important part of her life. As I got older, I understood more of what my parents did in the world. Still, on the outer edge of those important meetings or conferences they attended, I was confident that our family was the most important thing in the world to them. I never doubted that.

My parents chose lives of public service through politics. They didn't frame it as a sense of duty but rather as a responsibility. I was proud that my mother had worked to get legal help to people in difficult situations. She also volunteered at shelters for women trying to get themselves and their children out of abusive relationships. She took me along, when appropriate, and I would play with the kids there and, when I was older, I would help them with reading or homework.

My mother is also a woman of deep religious faith, and she believes that to be a good Christian is to do work that helps other people. She taught me that helping others is both a responsibility and a privilege and said nightly prayers with me, as did my dad.

My mom is always honest and loving. I remember one time in high school, I was working away on my physics homework. My mother said, "Chelsea, it's Friday night. You should be with your friends." I told her I had to do the work, or it would stress me out. She replied that it was good I wanted to do the work, but that I could do the homework tomorrow. My mother was showing me that it's good to be responsible but that you also have to take breaks from hard work and relax. I was sixteen, and, as usual, she was looking out for me.

As you can see, I was not a rebellious kid. My mom even had to prod me into taking a study break! I'm sure we had some conflicts at some point, but I don't recall us having a big fight we had to confront and reconcile. I think that comes from us being close and her making our relationship the main priority in her life, even when she had a very full schedule as First Lady. I've tried to do that with my own children. I want my kids to feel and to know, as keenly as I did, that they are the most important part of my life.

My mom's choice to make sure we were close and really knew each other was an important part of my childhood and even beyond.

I'm not proud of this particular event, but it tells you a lot about what I learned from my mother. When I was a freshman at Stanford, I called my mother hysterically crying and very upset.

I remember her being very concerned and asking what had happened.

I told her I had gotten a B minus on a chemistry test and started talking about how it was the end of the world.

There was a long pause. She said, "Okay. So, you are not in danger, and you are physically okay?"

"But, Mom," I said, "I'm gonna fail. This is awful news."

She then calmly told me a few things. B minus is not failing. And she said I needed to realize that I have a very good life, and I should really think about what is worth crying over. And, also, that I didn't want to be a chemist! I was taking the class in case I wanted to go to medical school. Not because I wanted to be the next Marie Curie!

Her words snapped me out of it. I admitted to the ridiculous nature of my overreaction and that the best thing to do would be to move on from this test and study harder for the next one.

Her handling of that phone call has always stayed with me. She knew me, so she knew what to say, knew what would help. She helped me get back on track quickly, and I think about how important that is for me to be able to do with my own children. I want to be for them what she was, and is, for me: someone I can turn to. Always.

Going across the country to Stanford was a wonderful adventure that I was ready for, but a real downside was that

I missed my parents. Being away from them showed me how close I felt to them.

When my dad ran for president, I was eleven and then turned twelve. It was a thirteen-month campaign, which seems quaint compared to today. That time was extremely busy for both of my parents, as they were constantly traveling and working day and night.

Yet, during that time, they made sure they either put me to bed or were there when I woke up. Right after the convention, I spent a week with one of my mom's good friends from college. But beyond that, there were only three other nights I wasn't with one or both of my parents. Think of the extraordinary commitment that took. I realize that they had a lot of resources and help but, still, the message to me was clear: Our family comes first.

My mother often uses an expression that she heard from her mother:

> *Life is not about what happens to you. It's about what you do with what happens to you.*

There are many examples of my mother doing just that in her role as my mother.

Have to work on a Saturday? Bring Chelsea with you.

Traveling endlessly while her dad is running for president? Get back to Chelsea as often as possible.

My mother spoke those words and lived them too. I've taken those words to heart and am proud to pass them on to my children. And, most importantly, to now live them— or aspire to live them—as a mom.

I also tell my children that for me, as their mom, the most important thing is for them to be brave and kind. My mother never said that those words to me, but she embodied them. I am so proud to be my mother's daughter and so grateful every day she is my children's grandma.

Photo Credit: Katie Couric

EVERYONE NEEDS A CHEERLEADER

Katie Couric

When my father, John Couric, died, *The Washington Post* published an obituary that would likely have irked him. It mentioned that he served in World War II, was a reporter for *The Atlanta Journal-Constitution*, and had worked in public relations for several trade associations. In the first paragraph, however, they referred to him as Katie Couric's father. In his life, whenever anybody said that to him, he would say, "Actually, she's my daughter."

A few years later, when my mother, Elinor Hene Couric, died, I called the same obituary writer at the *Post* who had written about my dad and told him that my mom had passed away. He said, "Well, what did she do?" I told him she volunteered for Planned Parenthood, worked in the gift department at Lord & Taylor, joined with some friends to arrange flowers for weddings and special events, and was also a stay-at-home mom who raised four successful and very nice people. After silence on the other end of the phone, he said, "We don't really do obituaries for people like your mom."

His remark made me realize just how undervalued mothers are—and made me think about the choices available to women of my mom's generation. My mom did not have a career outside our home, and for most women like her there were very few options. My mother was the CEO of our home and channeled all her ambition into making sure her four children had more options. She used to tell us, "Let 'em know you're there." She didn't want us to fade into the woodwork. She wanted more for us.

Born and raised in Omaha, Nebraska, my mother had an unmistakable Midwestern sensibility. She was very pragmatic, a no-nonsense kind of woman who had a lot of common sense. But outside our home, she was a bit shy and not exactly brimming with confidence. Though I never met my grandfather, she told me he often lost his patience with her. I don't think her parents propped her up the way she and my dad propped me up. She gave me what she didn't get, and I admire her so much for that. She used to say, "Everyone needs a cheerleader…and I'm yours."

Both of my parents were extremely encouraging, supportive, and took so much pleasure in any of their children's accomplishments, big or small. I feel I was loved so deeply and so unconditionally and have tried to be the same way as a mom. That kind of a solid foundation is so important, because it sets you up to deal with the challenges that life inevitably hands you.

As the fourth child and the baby of the family, I probably got away with more than my sisters and brother. I was the center of attention from an early age. My sisters would ask me to play the piano and do the splits when their dates would come calling, like some kind of trained monkey. I would happily oblige. No wonder I'm a natural performer. At the dinner table, I might say something bawdy and inappropriate, and my mom would laugh. My dad, trying not to laugh, would say, "Elinor, please don't encourage her," and shake his head. I loved making them laugh.

My mom gave me great advice. She told me that children, especially young ones, are satisfied with very little when they ask questions. "Less is more," she'd often tell me. When I asked about periods when she was driving me to my piano lesson, she gave me a very matter-of-fact answer. And that was that. This advice proved invaluable when my first husband, Jay Monahan, was diagnosed with cancer. During the nine months he was sick, our daughter Ellie asked me, "Is Daddy going to die?" I told her that I hoped he wasn't and that the doctors were doing everything they could to make him better. No false promises. The truth, plain and simple. Ellie nodded and went back to playing with her Barbie.

I also inherited my thriftiness from my mom. She grew up during the Great Depression and really appreciated the value of things. I'm the same way. I hate the idea of overspending or getting ripped off or being taken advantage of. I think I got that from my mom. But she was also very generous, and I think I am as well. Both my parents hated people who were pretentious or ostentatious. I'm like that too. I really don't like people who are showy or full of themselves.

Perhaps most importantly, though, my mom taught me to be present, as cheesy and new-agey as that sounds. As kids, the four of us never doubted that we were her number one priority. We always ate dinner together, and when I was raising my girls, it was really important for us to eat together just as I did growing up.

My mother died eleven years ago. When I think back on the most important thing she taught me, it was to love fiercely. For her, family was everything. That sentiment has been reinforced by the fact that my family has experienced more than our fair share of loss. But to never question how much you are loved is a real gift—something I appreciate more and more as I get older. That may not be worthy of an obituary, but it is worthy of my undying gratitude.

Photo Credit: Cindy Crawford

IF YOUR PARENTS WON'T TELL YOU THE TRUTH, WHO WILL?

Cindy Crawford

When people ask me to describe my mom, Jennifer Maki, I can't think of a better and more encompassing word than *mother*. The word truly embodies everything she is to me. She was a stay-at-home mom when we were little, and she was *everything*—she cooked, cleaned, tucked us into bed, drove carpool, and was our Girl Scout troop leader. During the summer, she even babysat other kids, at times being a mother to eight or nine children. She was a natural.

When I was younger, I used to call my mom a Pollyanna—not necessarily as a compliment. I would roll my eyes when she cheerily found the best in every situation. Only as I got older did I realize what a courageous choice that was—to live life looking for the good in everyone.

More than anything, my mother doesn't hold on to things. She moves forward, always seeing the glass as half full. Like most people, she's had hard times—losing my three-year-old brother, Jeff, to leukemia; going through a divorce; and living through years of stretching a paycheck to make sure there was milk on the table. But through it all, she chooses optimism. So, I suppose she *is* a Pollyanna, but I don't roll my eyes anymore.

Another word that describes my mother is *Midwestern.* She's a no-nonsense, meat-and-potatoes kind of woman. She grew up in a small town in Illinois, one of seven children. When you meet my mom, what you see is what you get. She has a self-deprecating sense of humor and an unshakable practicality. I remember before a family wedding, she joked, "I know my role—show up, shut up, and wear beige." It made us laugh, but there was truth in it. She's never needed to be the star of the show. She's comfortable in her own skin, happy to play her part without demanding attention.

When my parents split up a few years after my brother died, our house became one of four women—my newly single mom and her three teenage daughters. Besides the usual fights over clothes and the curling iron, my mom always made one thing clear: She was our *mother*, not our friend. She was strict—especially about curfew. For every minute we were late, we were grounded for a week. No ifs, ands, or buts. The only clock that mattered was the one on the microwave. Her reasoning? "Every minute of worrying why you're late feels like a *week*." This was before cell phones, so if we were late, she had no way of knowing if we were safe. To this day, I am *never* late.

We also had chores—*not* for allowance, but because we were part of a family. We were expected to contribute. We learned how to do laundry, vacuum, and even start dinner before my mom got home from work. When I was in third grade, my parents let me and my kindergarten-aged sister walk home for lunch. I'd make us grilled cheese and soup before we walked back to school. It was only a block, but the trust they placed in us gave me a sense of independence that stayed with me.

Losing a child is devastating for any family. But my mother helped us navigate that grief. Her strong faith gave her strength, and she leaned on our church community. She even took *Death and Dying* courses so she could help us process what we were feeling. She taught us to be grateful for the time we had with Jeff and to see his life as something that propelled us forward. She told us, "Jeff has done his job here. Now he gets to be with Jesus."

That was exactly what I needed to hear. Getting to be with Jesus made the idea of loss a little less heavy. Of course, we were devastated—we missed him terribly—but my mother kept us from getting lost in our grief. Her approach to my brother's death was a gift. She was the reason we could heal and keep moving forward.

It wasn't until I became a mother myself that I fully understood the depth of her loss. I remember calling her after my son was born and asking, "How did you do it? How did you survive losing a child?"

Her answer was so in line with who she is: "I had three other kids looking to me for guidance." So she got out of bed, made breakfast, and got us ready for school. That kind of strength still blows me away.

Having experienced loss early in life made me aware of how uncomfortable people can be around grief. Often, they say nothing for fear of saying the wrong thing. But my mother helped normalize it for us. Our church community surrounded us, prayed with us, and held space for our pain.

Years later, when my husband and I lost a close family friend, I called a therapist for guidance on how to help our kids through it. My mother had no therapist to call—she just instinctively knew how to comfort us. I trusted her then, and I still carry her wisdom with me.

More than anything, my mother's love was, and is, *unconditional.* My father, who loved us deeply, was more of a "reward for success and effort" kind of parent. My mother was different. She never tied love to achievement. Whether I got an A or a C, her love was constant. I appreciated that balance—knowing my dad would celebrate my straight A's, but also knowing my mother's love didn't waver, no matter what. That's the kind of love I want my own children to feel.

She was also incredibly supportive of my modeling career. I had been on a path toward becoming a chemical engineer, and while both my parents liked that idea, my mother encouraged me to explore modeling. She didn't say, "No modeling for you. You're a math and science girl." Instead, she said, "Try it. If you don't like it, you can come home and be right where you are now." No fear of failure—just encouragement. That unconditional love, again.

When I had the chance to go to Japan for work at seventeen, I was nervous. But she trusted me—and more importantly, she trusted her parenting. She had instilled independence in me, so when I found myself in Tokyo, living alone, I knew I could handle it. I earned $8,000 that trip, which felt like a fortune at the time.

Over the years, my mother has shared her parenting philosophy with me. She believes that the first five years are the most crucial—where you set the foundation. From five to ten, you reinforce those values. And after that? You're no longer the main influence in your child's life. "If you don't lay the groundwork early, you can't start parenting at sixteen," she told me.

Another thing about my mom? She never gives unsolicited advice. If she thinks you're being too lenient with your kid, she won't say a word—unless you ask. And if you *do* ask, she'll give you her honest opinion, usually prefaced with, "And if you don't want my honest opinion, don't ask."

I try to follow that same approach with my own children, but I'll admit—it's hard to hold your tongue. When my kids come to me with questions, I always ask, "Do you want my honest opinion?" They usually smile, bracing themselves for the truth. But that's the thing—if your parents won't tell you the truth, who will? Honesty, when it comes from love, should be valued, even when it's not what you want to hear.

Even now, my mother continues to teach me. One of the things I admire most is that she has never valued one of her children's accomplishments over another's. Because of my career, people often ask her, "How's your daughter?" referring to me. But she always responds, "Well, Chris did this, and Danielle did this."

I love that. She doesn't see my success as more important than theirs. And she has treated us all that way for as long as I can remember.

Because that's the kind of mother she is.

And I couldn't have asked for a better one.

Photo Credit: Henry Louis Gates Jr.

QUEEN FOR A DAY, MOTHER FOR LIFE

Henry Louis Gates Jr.

I was born in 1950, a time when television was beginning to take hold in America. The TV was on when I woke up until the time I went to bed. It was like the proverbial hearth, and we gathered around it. Nobody even thought of turning it off.

We had a nice TV, and nine channels, and that's just the way it was. It was a great start to my education because I was exposed to so many different things and ideas.

Some of my earliest memories of my mother, Pauline Coleman Gates, involve watching TV with her. My brother, Paul, was five years older than me and my dad worked two jobs in those early years, so it was often just Mom and me.

Before I started school, my mom and I watched those early predecessors of *Sesame Street*, *Ding Dong School* and *Romper Room*. In the afternoon, we watched soap operas. My education started with that time: with Mom and the conversations we had about what we saw on TV.

We also watched game shows, another staple of the early days of television. There was a show called *Queen for a Day*, and it was a show about giving a woman her own special day. You would go on the show and talk about your life, and the studio audience would vote one of the contestants to be the "queen" that day. You got invited on the show if someone nominated you.

One day, my mom and I were sitting and watching television when the phone rang.

This may sound irrational, but the ring had an urgency to it, like it was a special call. My mom answered the phone, and the caller said to turn the channel to *Queen for a Day*, and when she did, the host of the show was reading a letter that my uncle Harry had sent in nominating my mother.

We were so excited. Mom bought herself a nice dress and got to finally be on the TV that we watched so much. And that was the start of a nice time in my mother's life.

A few years later, my mother was selected as the first Black woman to be secretary of the local parent-teachers association in our town, Piedmont, West Virginia. Every month, all the Black people in the area would get dressed up in their Sunday finest to go to the PTA meeting and support my mother as she read the minutes of the previous meeting. She would wear that dress she wore on *Queen for a Day*. I'd look up at her, this goddess, who was reading those minutes so perfectly, and feel such pride.

Around this time, my mother started writing obituaries for Black people throughout the Potomac River Valley. When Mom found out someone had died, she would contact the family and gather some information about the deceased.

Then she would write an obituary that appeared in papers like the *Piedmont Herald* or the *Cumberland Times*. She also went to the person's funeral and would read the obituary as a eulogy.

My mother, this goddess, read for Minister McCall and the congregants these beautiful tributes. In my memoir, *Colored People*, I wrote that her eulogies described what you wanted to be in your heart, before the world corrupted you, before all the bruising that every human being takes because of the frustrations of lost dreams, dreams deferred, and ambitions never fulfilled. Her prose, and her reading of it, captured so much of the experiences and the lives of so many Black people in that region in those days. This part of my mother's life left an indelible mark on me, because I saw how her intelligence and sensitivity could soothe people in a sad time in their lives.

My mother, in the time I had her, influenced me in so many ways. First of all, she was a self-esteem machine. As we know, you can tell anyone that they are brilliant and beautiful and, after a while, they will believe it. My whole universe in those early years reinforced the idea that I was gifted and that my brother and I were going to be doctors or whatever we wanted. It never occurred to me that I was not the smartest kid in the class. I didn't need to take a test to know I was extremely capable in school. It wasn't a surprise that I went to Yale. She truly made me feel like a prince, like I was biologically blessed from birth.

My father used to say, "I love you boys, but not like your mother does. She'd beat up a tree if she thought it was offending you."

Everything changed in 1962. I was playing on the floor in front of the TV on a Sunday night, and my parents appeared in the room, all dressed up. They were very serious, and my mother essentially said that they were going to the hospital and that she was going to die. She told me she loved me, to be a good boy, and to take care of my father.

I cried like crazy, and she cried too. She was really convinced she was going to die. It had a fundamental effect on my psyche. I went upstairs to my room, and I prayed to Jesus that if he let my mother live, I would devote my life to Him. I cried myself to sleep, and I was miserable until Wednesday, when my mother came home, and it was clear she wasn't going to die.

It was one of the most emotional weeks of my life. And I did join a church to honor the promise I had made. I took it very seriously, and I didn't play cards or go to the movies or basketball games for a few years. But the thought of losing my mother was so profound that my reaction was in proportion.

In a way, however, I did lose her, though she lived until 1987. My mother's medical issues involved her reaction to menopause and the treatment she received in response to it. She was forty-six at the time, and her doctors put her on estrogen and other things. But that hormonal imbalance fundamentally transformed her personality. This once proud, brave, and bold woman became fearful and paranoid, and acted a bit strangely for the rest of her days.

Yet in some ways, she also remained a fantastic mom. She was a brilliant seamstress, and she always prepared us wonderful meals. But then she would say something rude to a relative, something you might think but would never say. She'd lost her filter. We all adjusted, and we still had her physical presence, but the woman I admired so—the writer, the orator, the secretary of the PTA—was no longer visible. The courageous woman who proudly—successfully—stood up to segregation in West Virginia schools had disappeared and was hiding inside the woman we now saw.

But after I matured and came into my own as a thinker and a writer, I saw my mother anew. It took me twenty-five years to realize it, but I had been living with my own James Baldwin, my model of a Black writer. My mother.

Photo Credit: Cass Bird Photography LLC

NOT TO BREAK MY FALL,
BUT TO HELP PICK ME UP

Kaia Gerber

My mother, Cindy Crawford, exists in multitudes. From my adult perspective, I view her not merely as an exceptional mother but as an extraordinary woman. Her role transcends the singularity of motherhood—a task she executes with seamless grace and profound empathy. The lessons she imparts today resonate as deeply as they did in my childhood.

Through her, I learned that identity resists confinement. "You don't have to accept the limits and labels that people may try to place on you," she would say, embodying this truth in her daily existence. We humans are complex, multifaceted beings—this understanding forms the bedrock of how I perceive her.

She is my mother. She is my confidante. These roles flow together in her presence, never mutually exclusive, shaped by her remarkable ability to evolve with my changing needs. She anticipates what I require before I can articulate it myself—this prescience, this silent knowledge, another demonstration of her wisdom.

The breadth of her accomplishments spring from an inexhaustible intellect and perpetual curiosity about humanity and the world it inhabits. Her interest in diverse subjects and people remains undiminished by time. Perhaps her greatest gift to me: this same sense of wonder. My open mind and constant searching exist as direct reflections of hers.

My mother's story intertwines with her own mother's narrative—a relationship I've been privileged to witness. They share a natural warmth, a welcoming radiance that disarms strangers. Their laughter carries that wicked Midwestern sensibility. I hope this quality lives in me too, despite my Los Angeles upbringing.

The summers of my childhood unfolded in DeKalb, Illinois, my mother's hometown, granting me profound appreciation for her origins. I came to understand the stark contrast between her youth and mine. Her backyard opened onto cornfields; mine faced the Pacific. That she preserved so many qualities from her upbringing and transmitted them to me so effortlessly, despite this environmental shift, reveals something essential about her character.

When she departed Illinois to pursue modeling, the world stretched before her largely unseen, with no guiding hand to illuminate the path. I stand privileged that when I entered that same industry, I had her to turn toward. Most who begin modeling lack access to someone who might reveal its inner workings. I admire how she navigated those early years independently, armed only with values her mother instilled in her and her own intelligence, judgment, and sense of self. When my turn arrived, that world did not feel foreign, because her support surrounded me.

Regarding my modeling career, she never pushed me toward it, just as her mother never pushed her. She remained adamant, repeatedly asking, "Do you want to do this?" My career unfolded organically beneath the shelter of her reassurance: "If at any point you are not having fun, you can always stop and reconsider." Her love created a safety net I will spend my lifetime trying to properly thank her for.

During my tender teenage years, her position remained steadfast: this should bring joy, nothing less. And truly, it did. I recognize the privilege of having a mother who doesn't live vicariously through me. Having experienced modeling's pinnacles and valleys herself, she felt no need to project her ambitions onto me. This allowed our relationship to deepen. Regardless of any outcome, I could describe my day and find instant understanding. Those mornings when we drove to work together, spent hours on set, hold particular significance.

At sixteen, I began working almost full time. My parents supported me as they would have, regardless of my pursuits. When I developed interests in stop-motion animation or dance, they invested time and resources into nurturing these inclinations. Their support would have manifested equally for any path I chose.

Among my mother's myriad qualities, her sincere compassion toward others stands paramount. She would take me on remarkable journeys when I was younger. At thirteen, we traveled to Peru to work with Orbis and their Flying

Eye Hospital, an organization providing essential eye care in regions where much blindness could be prevented through basic services.

In these environments, she is never passive. She enters with receptivity, eager to absorb the culture and history of places she encounters for the first time. We walked Machu Picchu, but we also visited hospitals, spending time with patients and their families.

I witnessed firsthand her open-heartedness. This wasn't performance—she is like the sun, rising and setting daily whether anyone observes its beauty or not. She appeared invariably supportive and kind, demonstrating genuine interest in those hospital proceedings. Her welcoming demeanor invited others to respond with matched open-ness. People visibly relaxed in her presence, feeling secure. I observed how she carried herself, and it imprinted upon me. I strive to greet others with similar openness.

Her strength and resilience define her equally well. The challenges of her youth became instruments through which she crafted better lives for my brother and me—not despite those difficulties, but because of them. My own resilient nature I credit entirely to hers. Bravery and courage charac-terize her too. I saw this when we returned to Peru with my brother and father. Traveling down the Amazon by boat, our guides captured an anaconda.

"Kaia, hold it!" she insisted.

"Are you insane? Absolutely not!" I protested.

Yet she persisted, and they draped it across my shoul-ders. While I screamed, she laughed. When they removed it from me, she took her turn. She has never demanded anything of my brother or me that she wouldn't require of herself. I understand now that with that snake, she attempted to instill something in me—risk-taking or boundary-pushing—qualities she embodies naturally. The photograph she took of me, tearful with an anaconda draped across my shoulders, now elicits only a smile and fond memories.

Her caring nature manifests in countless ways. Once during my childhood, on the day of my choir concert, work obligations called her away. Knowing its significance to me, she went to work, had her makeup done, then—with hair still in massive rollers—drove back to school to watch the performance.

The gesture moved me deeply, though perhaps I felt slight embarrassment at those rollers. In retrospect, I no longer see them. I see instead the dedication required to balance professional obligations with family priorities. Her example stands as testament to her motherhood.

Her compassion revealed itself equally when I encountered my first heartbreak. She sat beside me as we watched *Terms of Endearment*—a film I hadn't seen before. Words proved unnecessary; we simply cried together. She remained present through the experience, just as she had with the snake. Such presence became her gift. The first heart fracture remains unforgettable, but equally indelible is the memory of her hand in mine as we traversed that landscape together.

This story illustrates her consistent approach: granting me freedom to learn from mistakes and difficult situations. She wouldn't cushion falls or rectify problems, but her presence during recovery never wavered. She has given me perhaps life's greatest gift and our only non-replenishable resource: her time.

I feel grateful that she never attempted to mitigate pain or prematurely conclude natural processes. Even when she foresaw outcomes, "I told you so" never emerged from her lips. During overwhelming emotional periods, one often feels uniquely afflicted. My mother always countered, "I've made this mistake too. I know it hurts. But I'm glad you did it, because life isn't about avoiding mistakes. It's about learning and trying not to repeat them."

She doesn't retreat from fearful or difficult conversations. She taught me that the only way out is through. I know with absolute certainty that nothing I could reveal would drive her away or alter her perception of me. This certainty moves me to tears. She doesn't frighten easily and never hesitates to descend into feelings alongside you—a remarkable gift she extends to everyone she loves.

Her love often speaks through acts of service—one of her primary languages of affection. She performs small gestures for my brother, my father, and me that communicate her love. These actions emerge naturally from her being.

These acts assumed various forms throughout our lives. In childhood, they included fundamental caretaking: medical appointments, transportation, ensuring favorite foods, inquiring about our emotions.

Now, in our adulthood, she arrives and asks, "Have you eaten? Can I prepare something? "When visiting my home, she brings olive oil—somehow predicting I've run out. She avoids grand gestures, but these accumulated small attentions form the substance of unconditional love. She thinks of us constantly. It defies simple articulation, but I feel it and remain eternally grateful. Following her example, I perform countless small acts for those I love—my method of expressing affection.

Though I haven't yet had children, I hope to emulate her parenting approach. She never resorted to "Because I said so!" She invested time and patience in answering questions or alleviating fears. Frustration never led her to demand compliance without explanation. She wanted me to understand, recognizing that children's comprehension requires time. I treasure this aspect of her parenting and aspire to reproduce it. It provided me with unique understanding of my surroundings as I matured—a gift some children sadly aren't given. I want this for my future children. With increasing age comes deeper appreciation for the patience and care required to bestow such gifts.

Another bond we share: our love of reading. She remains one of few people I know who reads as voraciously as I do— perhaps more so.

Books perpetually occupy her hands. I completed my second-grade book report on John Steinbeck because she would read *Of Mice and Men* to me at bedtime. We've maintained our private literary society, discussing works by Joan Didion, Edith Wharton, and countless others. I hope someday to pass on this literary passion to my own children.

I've always known that my life's endeavor would be attempting to embody half her humor, kindness, compassion, and curiosity. Filling her shoes would be presumptuous—she has occupied them magnificently and continues to evolve within them. She never burdened me with expectations of living up to her example. My mother always maintained that sufficient abundance exists for everyone. "There is enough pie to go around. There is space for all of us." And I have my own shoes to fill—perhaps the most important lesson she has imparted.

Photo Credit: Steve Guttenberg

A CURVEBALL LIKE TOM SEAVER

Steve Guttenberg

My mother, Ann Guttenberg, was very young when she had me. She was just nineteen.

She had no idea how to take care of a baby, so much so that my grandmother Kate wouldn't let me, as an infant, leave her and my grandfather Sam's apartment for a month after I was born. My father was learning how to boil and sterilize everything while my grandmother taught my mom how to do everything "baby." Diaper, feed, heat food, take walks in the stroller, wrap me in so much wool that I had perpetual prickly heat.

At long last my grandparents let my mom and dad get their own apartment in Queens, and we moved there against my mom's desires. She loved to be home with her parents, especially when it came to having my grandparents watch over her as she learned motherhood with me.

I grew up in that Franklin Avenue apartment, a block off Main Street. There was a playground in the back that my father deemed "the snake pit," and I learned the pros and cons of street fighting. My father was a cop and wanted me to use my brain to disarm an opponent. My mother chose another approach: the fisticuffs, punch-the-other-guy-first school of fighting.

I practiced in our apartment with both my parents and used my abilities in the snake pit. I got a black eye once in a while but along the way gave a few shiners too. I remember my sister being pushed down a metal slide and knocking her tooth out. I was angry as hell, but my mom said that Sal, our upstairs neighbor, had pushed my sister by mistake. Mom taught me that not everyone gets a five-finger sandwich and to forgive is divine. Sal was spared.

One of my most cinematic memories was being in the snake pit when the ice cream man came out in front of the apartment building. Every kid ran to the back of the building, and every mother would put coins in a plastic bag and toss them out the window. It rained these plastic money pouches. My mother was no different, except she could throw a curveball like no one else. She was able to have our plastic bag of treasure coins sweep over the crowd and land deftly in my hands. I could tell which was Mom's, as it didn't drop straight; it sailed like a curveball from Tom Seaver. Some of my best catches were from my mom's golden arm.

At one point, my father announced at the kitchen table that we were moving to Long Island. He had just changed jobs, from being a police officer to working for my mother's cousin Harvey in electronics. My mom stood up and said, "That's not going to happen, Stanley! I love Queens, my friends are here, and my parents are in Brooklyn. I don't drive! I'm not moving!" We did, though.

We found a house in Massapequa, Long Island, and my mother learned to drive. But not without getting the car stuck in a bulldozer's catch her first two weeks on the road. She called my dad, and he came out and talked the cops into not giving Mom a ticket. "She's a new driver, guys; give her a break." From that moment on I saw that my dad was my mom's hero. That he would back her up, defend her, and be there for her anytime and in any situation. Even when her car got stuck on a bulldozer's mouth!

My mother is a proponent of common sense. She isn't against studying and school, learning and being educated, but for her nothing could replace good old-fashioned street smarts. The ability to smell out a situation. To know when to walk in or walk away. To suss out the personality of a stranger and know what his motives were. If he was a friend or a foe. My mother relies on a person's tenor, how they carry themselves. What they speak about, who their family is, the neighborhood they grew up in. Mom loves a "good-time Charlie," but knows to only trust him so much. She likes sincere types, bookish and smart, polite but not ass-kissing. She doesn't judge the privileged nor criticize the poor for lack of education. Mom loves to mingle in the upper crust but gets so much happiness out of having people to our house for coffee and cake after dinner. Her love of a good joke and a fascinating story is unmatched. Mom taught me to listen, to use my two ears and one mouth. To know when someone shows their true colors to believe them.

My mother has a feisty side, and she exhibited it on a sunny afternoon when my junior high school let out. Two of the most ferocious guys in ninth grade decided to fight it out in the schoolyard. The fight escalated to one where the black-leather-jacketed sharpie followed the denim-clad knife wielder onto the street and a pursuit occurred. The two ran with hundreds of kids behind them angling for a front-row seat. The two warriors landed in our front yard. Our front yard! They began to knife-fight with each other. My mother watched from the big bay window with my two sisters. I was one of the crowd in the street hoping that no one would recognize that it was my house where the heavyweight fight was taking place. All of a sudden, the front door opened, and my mother, her hair in curlers, ran out swinging an umbrella. "You kids get the hell off my lawn!" She started to swat the kids, especially the big ones in the crowd.

"Lady, shut up!" One of the bruisers grabbed my mother's umbrella and broke it in half.

"Oh yeah?" My mom gritted her teeth and spewed. She ran into the house, returning a few minutes later with my father's antique shotgun. The crowd saw this and fled like mice on a boat when the pirate cats pounce. The two kids who were fighting were left, and Mom helped them both up. And told them to shake hands and go home. Which they did. She then turned to me and said, "Son, that's how you break up a fight." I stood there, mouth agape. My mom knows how to fight!

During my high school years, I was especially close to my mom. She was my go-between to the opposite sex at Plainedge High School. I wasn't adept at talking to or even keeping eye contact with girls, and in ninth and tenth grades I found myself standing alone at the dances, or not going entirely. Then, in eleventh grade, my workouts in our basement weight room with my dad and the high calorie input from my mom's cooking started to blossom. I got muscles. Muscles in muscles. And that's the currency in most high schools. I got noticed by the delights of the class of '76, and also the classes younger and older. I began to date one of the prettiest girls, and I had everything but game. I couldn't get any words out that would charm her other than my physical looks. So, Mom educated me on the vocals, on the language of love, the romance, and the flowers in a sentence. Mom and I sat up for hours talking about the differences between men and women. How they are opposites, yet they come together as a whole. Mom gave me her thoughts on how a couple behaved and that not every day will be a party. That's it for better or for worse. That a couple has to be able to be one and also be individuals. That my grandparents lived and worked together. That their honeymoon was going to the movies and having chocolate-covered cherries. That it doesn't take money to be in love, it just takes love.

I eventually moved to LA to pursue my dream of being an actor. My mother wasn't big on the idea, but she knew my drive. I wanted it more than anything. My parents gave me two weeks to become a movie star. I worked like a fiend and nabbed a Kentucky Fried Chicken commercial. That proved to my parents that I had a chance. It was very hard for both of them to let me stay in California and try my hand at show business. My mother always told me I could take my marbles and come home. That being a movie star wasn't as important as being happy. That life is to be lived with laughter and love, that the superficial isn't what makes a birthday. It's who is there to help you enjoy it. I've stayed for forty years now. And I always remember that I can take my marbles and go home any time I want.

Photo Credit: Laura Jarrett

YOU'LL BE FINE

Laura Jarrett

"You'll be fine...." These are the words so often repeated by Valerie Jarrett whenever I fall—literally and figuratively. We lovingly call it her life mantra. Whether it's a stumble on a sidewalk, lipstick on your teeth, a failed relationship, or a major job change, the response from my mother is consistent. As a kid, I used to mistake the phrase as being dismissive or a refusal to acknowledge the gravity of my perceived problem, or a by-product of parental exhaustion. But what I failed to understand at the time was that she was building me up with the most valuable gift of all: resilience.

My mother is the strongest person I know, some of which undoubtedly must be because her own mother was extraordinary. Raised at time when our society and laws sought to put limits on how high a Black woman could climb, Barbara Bowman forged her own path. And she taught her only daughter, Valerie, through example and action, to do the same. Born in Iran, with fair skin, red hair, and an English accent from her early travels, Valerie didn't look or sound like anyone else around her when she arrived on Chicago's South Side as young girl, but her mother sent her off into the world, always saying, "You'll be fine." And she was, even when it didn't go exactly according to her plan. Over the next sixty years she would go on to the finest schools, practice law at major firms, marry, have a baby who she'd raise as a single parent, climb the ranks in city government, achieve great success in corporate America, and end up being the longest-serving senior adviser to the president of the United States. Turns out she was more than fine.

As an adult and parent now myself, I believe my mother's mantra may have also served as her reminder to herself when she needed to be brave for the both of us. Sometimes as parents we pretend to be fine, even when we aren't and don't know what comes next. We have to show up for kids so they can feel confident, even when we are feeling unsure. She didn't set out to raise a child on her own with a demanding full-time job—that wasn't the plan. And when my father passed away when I was eight, she didn't have a playbook for that. But that quickly became her reality, so she adapted.

Part of what my mother would say she learned over time is that a "plan" is only that—it may be a good intention, but it's not the end of the story. Early in life so often we find ourselves reaching for the next goal post, but passing too quickly over the value of the journey and what's learned along the way. My mother's mantra tries to take all the many mistakes and missteps of life in stride instead of a reflection of failure. So, whenever a crack in my own plan has cropped up in life—be it a bad grade or a bad boyfriend—"You'll be fine" is her way of reminding me that all was not lost. It's her spin on "Don't sweat the small stuff." And to be clear, it hasn't always been well received. When I was a little girl and terrified of rollercoaster rides, the "You'll be fine" phrase did not solve the pit in my stomach. Or when my face was swollen to the size of a chipmunk from a wisdom tooth extraction, and I was nevertheless sent off to the tenth grade looking like something from *The Nutty Professor* (because God forbid, I miss a day of school)—I was less than inclined to find the "You'll be fine" mantra helpful. Or there was that time we found ourselves in the middle of a hurricane on vacation. Not heeding the evacuation orders, we were left to ride it out. I was skeptical, but she assured me that we'd be fine, and thankfully, she was right.

She applies the mantra equally to actual hurricanes or hurricane-like changes in life. When I decided to take the plunge from a fruitful career practicing law for the unknown waters of broadcast journalism, I was grateful for my mother's approach. She could have hit me with a dozen reasons I was making a mistake. But she has never once wavered in her commitment to having my back. That doesn't mean that she doesn't ask questions. She has *plenty* of opinions. But she has always encouraged me to chase the things in life that fuel and excite me—even if the route is circuitous, *especially* if the route is circuitous. She doesn't want me to live in fear, and she somehow figured out that the more support she provides, the less space there would be for self-doubt to creep in. I wasn't entirely sure my career switch was going to work, but I was 100 percent confident that even if it failed miserably, I'd be just fine. Her mantra works like an emotional safety net.

Sometimes my mother says, "You'll be fine," without any words at all, just with her eyes. When my son was a few months old and I was at the end of my rope with hours of failed breastfeeding and his screaming and I really wanted to cry myself, she knew that if she said, "You'll be fine," I probably would have snapped at her. Instead, she gave me "the look," her patented silent version of the mantra—imparting strength when I desperately needed it. When my newborn daughter had RSV at a time when so many other children were ending up hospitalized, I tried to remain calm and found myself repeating the mantra silently. And I find myself now saying it out loud to my own children, whether they appreciate it or not. My mother is with me even when she doesn't know it.

When my grandmother passed away, I wondered if we would be fine. I often think of how she would handle a situation or what she would say. I know she would tell my mother and me that will be fine. Thankfully, my mom and I can look at each other, without saying anything, and know that is true.

Photo Credit: Noah Kahan

THE REAL GOLDEN RULE

Noah Kahan

"You don't have to like everyone, but you have to be kind."

And that was that. Arguing with my mother, Lauri Berkenkamp, about the validity of this particular aphorism would be about as fruitful as mowing a lawn by picking each blade of grass with tweezers, one at a time. There is an understanding that by the time you'd plucked each plant from its root, the yard would have regrown, and there have to be better ways to waste time.

My mother's belief in kindness was too firmly planted to be disrupted by my challenges of "But what if they really suck?" and "Even if they're a serial killer?" I knew what she meant. Kindness was a sacred pillar in her worldview and an undeniable constant in the way my mother approached the world. She spread it out not only amongst four rambunctious and occasionally *unkind* children but also to the friends, neighbors, and complete and total strangers that interloped through our lives in small-town New Hampshire.

Even at my most surly and my least kind, my mom would stay strong and provide a living and sometimes confounding example of the power of generosity and understanding. As I watched her navigate a world in which everyone deserved the benefit of the doubt, I would wonder, *"How can everyone deserve kindness?"* There are so many assholes. Why should I smile at the moron throwing his trash out of his car window and littering the forest? Why shouldn't I honk at the dipshit texting on his phone in the left lane going fifteen miles under the speed limit? I couldn't understand it. An old poster in my elementary school classroom boasted the famous golden rule: Treat others how you want to be treated. In my head, I could only understand the logic of treating others the way they treated you. My mom, though, did not feel the need to wait for permission. She lived by her rule. You have to be kind.

Looking back, it was a very special and powerful form of kindness to endure the drone of my persistent and seemingly impossible dream. To sit and nod your head with approval as a nine-year-old boy loudly tells you, "I want to be a rock star." To listen to screechy, depressing "songs" come out of his bedroom, or the kitchen, or *her* bedroom, at full volume, out of key, every day, and to continue to let him believe in his naive dream. It was probably embarrassing to watch me hand out burned CDs to aunts and uncles, who would play along to not hurt my feelings but would scratch their heads at the title of my debut album, *Death to the Lord*, and wonder, *What the hell does that mean?* (By the way, I still have no idea, but I can understand why my parents wanted me in therapy from a young age.) My mom never told me, "You suck," which I probably did. She never told me, "This is annoying," which it probably was.

I would not blame my mom if she thought every hour of every day that I was never going to be a rock star, or a singer, or even a working musician. I wouldn't blame her if she cut up the quarter-inch cables attached to the old Fender amp and replaced them with the schoolwork I never cared to do. It would have been a logical response to an irritating sound. Most people swat mosquitoes when they buzz around their heads. She never swatted my dream away. She didn't harbor any ill will at me for deciding not to utilize the opportunity I was born into, that she and my dad had worked so damn hard to provide us kids with. We were in the best school, in the nicest town, had a clear passage to any traditional form of success, and I decided I'd rather strum on my cherry-red Stratocaster. I'd like to think she saw incredible potential in my out-of-tune singing and morbid writing, but I think the early days of my dream existed solely because of her rule. It was the kind thing to do.

I like to believe she felt a sense of karmic justice when I actually started to get kind of good. I like to think she heard the first piece of music that had a clever rhyme scheme, or the first melody that got stuck in her head, and looked up toward God or whichever saint and said, "Told you! I was nice enough to endure it when he sucked, and now I've got his damn song stuck in my head!" I have never asked her about when she first realized I might have developed the talent to match my insatiable and almost religious passion for music, and if she felt partly responsible. She was. She was the lamppost and inspiration for me in so many ways. My mom is an extraordinary writer and the biggest music fan I know. I tried so hard to sound like the artists that she would listen to, imagining in my head my song coming up on shuffle and her listening to it like it belonged in a playlist next to Paul Simon, The Avett Brothers, or Crosby, Stills & Nash. I tried to write in a prose that seemed mature enough to exist on the same shelf as one of her bestselling books. I wanted to be good enough to satisfy the greatest musical taste I knew, and I wanted her to mistake my writing for her own.

She would give me advice on writer's block, on rediscovering creativity during the many times it eluded me, and she would edit and evaluate my songs. Occasionally, during my mid-teens, I would be stuck on a certain word, unable to figure how to complete a rhyme while staying within the parameters of the larger lyrical concept. I would roll it around in my head and on my tongue for hours, literally banging my head against my desk until I could no longer think without my brain hurting. I would wander downstairs, distracted, and my mom would ask what I was working on up in my bedroom. I'd tell her I was stuck on a word to complete a rhyme, and then I'd speak out the problem lyric to her. Almost instantly she would have the answer. I like to think she enjoyed the exercise of writing "with me," so to speak. That she enjoyed the teaching and the helping and the editing and the encouraging. She taught English at the University of Vermont and wrote thirteen books, so maybe her writing advice was just an extension of her training and expertise, the natural instinct of a highly trained professional who sees an overly critical amateur trying to skip the hard parts of writing and creating—to lend her hand and guide them through the inevitable, toward improvement and toward confidence. Part of me hopes she loved that partnership as much as I did, but part of me is sure that even if she couldn't stand it, she would have done it anyway. She was never partisan in her total love for me and my siblings, whatever wild dream it was we were chasing in those meandering teenage years.

However, without any doubt, it was kindness and not passion that saw my mom through the "grind years" of my journey to becoming a full-time musician. Three times a week, after working a full day at the library, my mom would pick me up and drive me to one of the several local restaurants that offered locals a chance to play covers or originals at their open mic nights. Hanover, New Hampshire, was a small town, and on weeknights, when the Dartmouth students were studying for their rocket ship classes or whatever, these restaurants were almost always completely empty, save for a few locals who seemed to want nothing more in the world than for the music to be turned down to an indecipherable volume and for the musicians to let them enjoy their food in peace. (Why they would choose to consistently eat out on an open mic night is beyond me, but I digress.)

My mom would sit in the back of the dark and noisy bars, focused so intently as I performed my cover of "Creep" by Radiohead or "Trouble" by Ray LaMontagne. She'd heard each about a thousand times but would sit and watch, nonetheless. She would afterwards tend to the wounds of my ego, when a record executive didn't magically happen to be eating at Salt Hill Pub that night, or when the sound of silverware on plates was the only reception to my performance. She would encourage me by finding a positive no matter how bleak I felt, and by unlocking the front door of her car, time and time again, to bring me to the next one. It must have been exhausting for her to work all day, be present and supportive to three other children and a various number of dogs, and then to emotionally uplift a distressed seventeen-year-old singer-songwriter. I wish I could have been more grateful at the time.

It wasn't until years later, after the record deal, the Wikipedia page, the "Oh shit, we fucking did it!" moments that could I fully appreciate the kindness that carried me here. It wasn't until my mom was thousands of miles away from me that I realized how badly I needed that encouragement growing up. Sometimes, even thousands of people screaming the words to your songs can sound like a blank sheet of paper and an emptier brain. Sometimes, even Madison Square Garden can feel like an empty bar in Lebanon, New Hampshire. When it does, I try and tell myself that if my mom could sit and watch me squeak out a Kendrick Lamar cover (I know) and drive me home on a Wednesday in the February dark, or the April slush, or the oppressive August heat without giving up, then I could find the strength to keep going too. I could use the proof of her love for me as a way to find my own love for what I was doing and could use that belief as a reason to keep going.

Kindness doesn't cost us anything. I sometimes fall into thinking I am unworthy of even being kind to myself. That I should not give myself the benefit of sympathy or understanding, that life is a zero-sum game, and if I have failed or lost then I am simply existing in the consequence of a cold and definitive world, and that painful feeling of failure is the result. Today, I try to remember the greatest lesson my mother ever taught me: Kindness should be a given. Kindness should be shown to the surly stranger on the highway, for who knows what tribulations they have been through in their day or week or life to lead them into your own path. There doesn't have to be a reason. In fact, when it feels least appropriate, or when you're at your most irritated, that is when kindness is most important.

In a world that presents so many opportunities to judge and deny and disregard, I remember my mother's rule. Love you, Mom.

Photo Credit: Hoda Kotb

YOU CAN DO IT!

Hoda Kotb

ow in the world my parents juggled raising two children and attending college—as immigrants from Egypt—I'll never know. It's both a mystery and a miracle to me. At Oklahoma University, my dad was earning his doctorate, my mom her master's, all while wheeling kids around and navigating the American dream. After graduating from OU, they moved my sister, my brother, and me to Morgantown, West Virginia, where my dad landed a teaching job.

West Virginia rocked! We loved it. Not only did we sing John Denver songs, to this day, "Take Me Home, Country Roads" is still my mom's favorite song. We lived on Dogwood Avenue with what seemed like a hundred kids on our street because there were so many families. It felt like the perfect childhood, in a perfect setting, where kids could run free or go sledding down the street, and there were always friends nearby.

Of course, not everything was perfect. In elementary school, people would ask me, "How do you pronounce your name?" During roll call, I used to shrink down in my seat and cross my fingers. *Oh, please just get my name right.* To teachers, "Hoda Kotb" must have looked like a land mine right after they'd breezed through "Susan Keller." I would flop sweat because everything was so atypical about the Kotb family. Together, we were known as "cop bees." Eventually, everything worked out. The beauty of living in a small town is that even if you're different, over the years people get to know you and the oddball status fades away. Before you know it, you're just another neighbor humming a John Denver tune.

Throughout our childhood, my parents would teach us, "This is the land where you can do anything. If it doesn't work out for you in this town, it can work out someplace else." That's not the case in Egypt. There, you can have a doctorate degree, work hard, and still not get a particular job because you're not from the right place. My parents believed that America offered an equal playing field, and my mom, Sami, still believes it to this day. She says that if you work hard, there's a place for you. You just have to find it.

Sami was always a cheerleader for us as kids and continues to be to this day. She's two pompoms and a "You can do it!" Talk about someone being "born on a sunny day"—that's her. No matter what, she always thinks the day is going to be bright. I recall her looking outside on a cloudy day and saying, "You know, it looks like it might be sunny later." That's how she is! She's a lifelong optimist.

Sometimes I would get a text from her in the morning after the *Today* show, brimming with her usual warmth. "My God, you look beautiful this morning." "Al Roker is so funny." "I love your outfit." To this day, my mom picks out many of the clothes I wear. She has a great eye! Whatever outfit she selects at Nordstrom, she sends me in a box. I would pick it up and take it to work without ever opening it first because it always fits.

I know how fortunate I am to have such a loving mother. Her support throughout my life has been good for my well-being and has made me feel like I could do anything. She's the same way with my daughters, Haley and Hope. To watch her play with them and whisper encouraging words to them is a dream come true. She'll say, "Oh, these girls are *amazing*! Look at *this* drawing!" I not only remember when she said those things to me, but I also remember how I felt. "Mom, look!" I'd say before jumping off the edge of the pool. "Oh, that was *incredible*," she'd gush. To her, everything was exceptional and amazing. While some people say you can overpraise your kids, I just don't think so if your input is authentic. My mom's positive words have always sprung from her soul; she truly believes them, and she's not just trying to make someone feel good.

When people meet Sami, they say, "Hoda, you are just like your mom!" (I hope so!) I certainly am a cheerleader, too, and have been since I was a little kid. I love that role. It's better for me to be cheering for the person winning than to be the person winning. That's not because I don't like to win, but I like to be on a team, to be part of something. I'm inspired by the energy of a group. When we moved to DC, I joined the school basketball team and loved it. From the court, I really experienced Mom's optimism and hope. We could be down eight points with three seconds on the clock and my mom would still believe. I would too! I'd think, *If I could take a shot, I could draw the foul. That would be three points.* I would play the imaginary game in my head and get eight points in no time. Sometimes what we imagine does happen! Her optimism was something I soaked up and now live by in my own life. After all, staying positive is a much more fun way to move through the world than the alternative.

Mom also believes she can complete anything she tries. When she turned sixty, she decided that she was going to run the Marine Corps Marathon in Washington, DC. My brother, my sister, and I were all there to watch her try. It turned out to be a crazy hot day in November—75 or 80 degrees. Too hot for a marathon. We met her at different points along the route, and at mile six, Mom was sweating and looking drained. My sister decided that one of us needed to get into the race and help her out. However, my sister had on flip-flops, and my brother had on something akin to topsiders. Because I was wearing sneakers, I said, "Okay, I'll go," and I jumped in with her. We start running and talking and somehow completing mile after mile as we cruised along together.

There's a point in the Marine Corps Marathon—at mile twenty-one—that if you don't reach it by a certain time, they open up the road to traffic. That means you must leave the race, get on a bus, and ride to the end. It happens at around 2:30 or 3:00 p.m., and I knew our timing was getting tight. I urged, "Mom, we've got to get there. It's close."

But we arrived a bit too late, and the highway was already back open. A policeman pointed to a bus and told us to get on it, and we could see other people onboard. But we'd come this far, and I said to my mom, "We're running." Her face was like, "What??" I demanded, "We are going on!" We ran past the policeman and onto the highway. I remember the cars whizzing by us. My mom was squealing, but we finally got to the bottom of the Iwo Jima Memorial, where the finish line is set up. I stopped at the bottom, and my mom ran up to where the Marine Band plays. She finished while I stood at the bottom of that hill with my towel. My brother was at the top with my sister. I was crying, my sister was crying, and my brother was crying. Wow! She did it! And I'm standing there thinking, *Oh my God*. My mom couldn't believe it either and loved that we had all witnessed it. It was one of those forever moments.

Now, whenever there's something I don't think I can do—whatever it may be—I remember that hot day. I remember how she ran the marathon at age sixty. Who knows if she was ready; I don't think she was. Yet, she finished. And I remember it now as one of the most significant ways she mothered us—by just finishing a race. She didn't quit. She didn't walk off. She didn't say, "Well, that was a dumb idea."

I think about that can-do approach with my own kids. It's what you do, not what you say. Instead of telling our kids to finish things, just finish things. Instead of asking our kids to be polite, just be polite. Our little ones are watching us day and night, so it's up to us to walk the walk.

Most of the things I've overcome and accomplished in my life are because of my mom. She was one person who always said I could do it. The one person who believed in me against all odds. The idea that that I would wind up as cohost of the *Today* show is nuts. If someone was in Las Vegas and asked, "What are the odds that this kid from Morgantown, West Virginia, would ever end up in Rockefeller Center cohosting the *Today Show*?"—they would be a million to one...or even more unlikely. But when I landed my first job in broadcasting, my mom said to me, "Well of course they're lucky to have you in Mississippi!" And then I'd head to my next job, and she'd tell me, "Oh, you now work in Moline, Illinois? What a beautiful spot." I just kept moving, and she kept falling in love with the cities and telling me how amazing they were. She'd say, "Oh my gosh, did you see this restaurant?" I watched how she made every place someplace to love. And she was like that when I moved to New York City. I was intimidated, but my mom would ask me during a visit, "Did you meet the nice man who runs that kiosk downstairs? He knows how I like my coffee now." I thought, *You already know him??!* I watched her make a community wherever she went.

What beautiful lessons I've learned from my mom, including the fact that you don't need everyone to believe that you can do something. You just need one. I truly believe that if you have just one person who wholeheartedly believes in your excellence—even if you haven't already achieved it—it's amazing what you can do. I keep thinking about that for my girls. I'll whisper, "Hey, Hope, what are you going to do?" "Mama," she'll say, "I'm going to change the world!" She's just six. My eight-year-old, Haley, says the same thing. Now, are they really going to change the world? We'll see. But you can bet I've got my pompoms out, cheering them on at whatever they do, as we share our sunny—or soon to be sunny—days together.

Thank you, Mom.

Photo Credit: Téa Leoni

THE BEST KIND OF SUPERHERO

Téa Leoni

I think that there are moments when you really come to "know" your mother. There are these extraordinary "aha" moments when you realize the person that she truly is. It's not what she says, but what she *does*. The way she moves in the world.

My mother, Emily Patterson, is a Texan. She was adopted, and family has always been the most important thing to her. My grandmother tells the story of how the hospital called her and said, "We have a little girl for you." So, Grandmom and Granddad got all dressed up and made the journey to the hospital in San Antonio. The two of them sat on this bench while they brought out this baby girl, and Grandmom looked at her and said, "That's not my baby." She gave this baby *back*, and they returned to the train and went home to Austin. Two years later, they got another call, and they made the same journey, to the same hospital, and sat on the very same bench. This time, when they brought out this newborn, Grandmom said, "Now, that's my baby girl!"

My mother is a basket of beautiful contradictions. She was a piano prodigy, and by age fourteen she was playing some of the best Chopin anywhere in Amarillo. She was a straight-A student. At the same time, she learned how to drive a car at thirteen and was secretly drag racing the next year. She will set a table that looks like the most magnificent thing in the world, but she's also a great partyer and not afraid to "trash the table" and be the first one to do it. I've got pictures of her with her bare legs on top of that table, white wine in one hand and red in the other. I mean, my mother is *surprising*. You just can't put her in a box and label her. If I've ever been surprising, it's only because I learned it from her.

Mind you, Mom will never ask for or expect an accolade. She never wants to stand up and take credit for something or get an award. I swear it's probably why she never plays the lottery because, God forbid, she'd be the winner and become the focus of something! And she never complains, ever. Even when she was going through some life stages that women go through, my mother never talked or complained about a hot flash. She has knees that are pretty much bone on bone at this point, and she walks at least ten miles a day. I've maybe heard her talk about an ailment twice, like when she broke both of her arms a few years ago and was in two enormous casts. She was up on Cape Cod with these big cast claws on her arms—we called her "Lucy the Lobster." Yet, she was still walking ten miles a day with these huge things on, and she never complained.

I was born in New York, we did time in New Jersey, and we returned to New York City when I was ten. There were not many Texans living in New Jersey. I have a brother, and we were a very tight family unit. I love the way Mom raised us. She was tough. She was totally loving. She didn't bend very easily. She would say the rule once, and that was it. However, I do think that my mother was more concerned about my growing up to be strong than she was about my brother doing so. She taught me that life isn't always fair, and her view of the world is that women need some grit. Grit is important.

Mom also has a very strong connection and commitment to justice. That sense of justice, and my first "aha" moment, came when we lived in New Jersey. We had a great neighborhood and gang of kids, but there was this one bully—he was such a bully. I mean, he was something straight out of central casting. He had this burnt-red hair, and he even rolled the sleeves of his t-shirts like a like a '50s bad boy version of Fonzie. I was probably seven and he was probably thirteen, and he was a big kid. He used to whale on me and another friend because we were the youngest.

One day, I was in our front yard, and this bully was swinging me around and then letting me go. I was getting hurt right in front of our house, and my mother saw it and came out. She let out this guttural yell, took off her penny loafer, held it over her head, and started chasing after this kid! Right in front of me and a couple of others. We'd never seen anything like it! So, we ran after my mom, who's running down the street, around the corner, on the sidewalks, chasing this bully. She came into this kid's yard. I'd never even been in the bully's yard—nobody went in that yard. He must have beaten her there and got inside his front door. My mom ran up to the front door and banged on it with her loafer and then just stood there. I think she'd forgotten that she had her shoe in her hand. Suddenly the door opened, and this huge demon of a guy, with this dingy t-shirt on, was just filling up the whole doorway. At this point, all of us kids were hiding behind a bush, and I honestly thought my mom was going to be dead. I was panicked. This guy just looked at her, and Mom put her shoe down. I don't know if she said anything to him, but he slammed the door in her face, and she was left standing there. We were all shocked. I remember running back home so that Mom wouldn't see us hiding there. After that, she was kind of a legend in the neighborhood. It was a big story that this hotheaded Texan had chased the bully out of our space and squared off against his huge demon of a dad.

Now, my brother and I never thought about *why* this kid was such a bully. The thought that he had anybody who loved him, let alone parents, was so far beyond our imagination. We never even bothered to wonder about it. And the fact that he had this demon tucking him in at night was now just an extraordinary thought for us.

About three weeks later, I got off the school bus, and as I was walking up to my house, I saw my mother sitting on the front stoop with this same boy, and he had his schoolbooks out in front of him. I just stopped and watched him and my mom. I guess she was tutoring him. I'll never, ever, forget that. I don't remember talking to my mom about it right then, but I became aware that she continued to see him. He never messed with any of us again. Ever. Years later, I talked about it with her, and she told me that as soon as she met the dad, she understood the kid. But it was so extraordinary to me, and it was just her. I don't judge easily or quickly, and that is because of who my mother is. She taught me that you have no idea what's going on in someone's life, or what their life has been, or whether at some point they knew great pain. She believes that you have to respect everybody. I know that she changed that kid's life.

Now, many years later, when I was an adult, Mom and I were in a big-box store, Target. We were roaming the aisles, and there was a girl. This sort of Raggedy Ann child, probably about eleven or twelve, and on the cusp of puberty. She was sort of coming out of her clothes, which were too small for her. It was clear that this family was hurting a little bit. Her parents, but it may have been her grandparents, were jerking her down the aisles by grabbing her wrists. In my entire life, my mother never grabbed my wrist. She held my hand. We could hear them talking to her. It was partly audible, but we didn't know precisely what was being said. And this child was just standing there looking sort of stunned and numb and going along. I suppose we crossed them again in different aisles.

Eventually, I went somewhere else in the store to pick something up, and I lost my mom and went looking for her. I came around one of these aisles and saw that my mother was squatted down, and she had her hand just gently on this girl's arm. She told her, "You stay tough. You stand up. You're all right. You're going to be fine. Someday you're going to be free."

I just burst into tears, and it was almost like that moment from so many years ago. I sort of ducked back behind, not the bushes this time, but around the other aisle, and I just broke down. I couldn't believe what I just heard. How did she have that moment? It had to have been almost a split second of an opportunity and decision. She took it and said this profound thing to this child and then just wiped away this kid's tears and stood up. I was speechless. I think at this point, the idea solidified in me that my mother was the best kind of superhero, because she was the private superhero. She didn't wear some kind of gaudy cape and fly. No one ever really saw or knew what she did. She was like a mirage of a superhero.

Sometimes I think other people teach their kids to respect the people who *they* respect. My mother makes it clear that you should have respect for everybody. She treats everybody like they are valuable. Worthy. And possibly better than she is. I don't mean that she puts herself down, I mean that she looks at everybody as a "possible." I realize that she gave me that gift. Mind you, she never said this. She never sat me down and said, "Now listen, you need to treat people this way." I just see the way she moves in the world. There is no bravado to her. She doesn't have to do that. The great thing about her is her combination of toughness, shrewdness, morality, and decency. And it's so very powerful.

Photo Credit: Tatyana McFadden

THEY CHOSE ME TO BE THEIR DAUGHTER

Tatyana McFadden

I am the lucky one. I have two moms. And they chose me to be their daughter.

I was born in 1989 in St. Petersburg, Russia, with a condition called spina bifida, which left me unable to move or feel my legs. When I left Baby Orphanage #13, it was with a grim prognosis. I managed to beat the odds thanks to Deborah McFadden, former commissioner of disabilities for the USA (1989–1993), who came to the orphanage on an official visit. I was six years old at the time and had watched other children be selected by their "parents" and move on to a better life. And though I cannot explain it, I knew with 100 percent certainty that Deborah (whom I called my "mamochka") was going to be my mother. And I was right.

An important part of our story is that older kids in orphanages or kids with disabilities are often not visible on visits from outsiders. People want to see the younger, generally healthier kids. Even at six, I was considered older, and I had my physical issues. I was off in the corner as usual. The staff at the orphanage had not even planned to take

Deborah to the room where I was, but she said, "I want to see all of this." Those words, which tell you a lot about Deborah, started our family.

It is impossible to describe the "magic" of America and my new family. While it seemed like one big adventure to me, to my parents (Bridget O'Shaughnessy is my other mother) it was, literally, a fight for my life. I was malnourished and not expected to live, so the doctors suggested my parents build as normal a life as possible. And so, they did. My life began to include sports programs, Girl Scouts, nutritious food, play dates with friends. It seemed simple to me, but behind the scenes, both of my parents, from the very beginning, had to fight for my rights.

Those fights hit the front page when I discovered wheelchair racing and started to compete on a national and international level. After I was denied the right to race alongside other members of my high school track team, I turned to my parents. They led the charge, suing Howard County, Maryland, for my right to race alongside able-bodied runners. Their courage led the way to victory, changing forever the face of high school athletics in my town, my state, and throughout the United States.

As I was growing up, it was my parents who woke at dawn to accompany me on my workouts. Trips to competitions often became their vacations. Family plans were changed to accommodate my schedule. And when I was diagnosed with a life-threatening blood-clotting disorder, they were with me, encouraging me, believing in me, and doing everything they could to help me achieve my dreams, regardless of personal sacrifice.

My moms are loving, warm, dedicated, devoted, genuine, caring, creative, determined, and fun. They both managed careers while raising three adopted daughters, two with disabilities. We were quite the sight. Two moms, three daughters, one in a wheelchair, one with a prosthetic leg—a nontraditional family in every way. Fighting discrimination was what they did to defend the rights of their daughters. If they faced personal challenges, because of their relationship, I was unaware.

They actually met "on the track" in the 1980s. Debbie, recovering from the devasting effects of Guillain-Barré syndrome and still using crutches, signed up to participate in a "fun run" to support the 1984 Summer Olympics. Bridget, already a runner, volunteered to help Debbie run the race. And they have been running ever since. Running a home, running a family, running a business, and running with me!

Both of my moms are strong, powerful, and loving. They are also distinct from each other, in many ways. If I need an equipment change on one of my racing chairs or I need to change a tire, I'll go to Bridget. She's the tool master. She can fix anything and could build a house on her own if she wanted. Bridget is also a bit more athletic and outdoorsy, and she'll work out with me and train with me. In high school, I remember working out late at night with a headlamp on, and Bridget was right there with me.

If I have a business question, say about a contract or sponsorship, I'll go to Debbie. She monitors my career and helps me navigate the various parts of it. But I also have many memories of Debbie at the track. They would alternate being at a race or practice with keeping things working at home.

The early part of my athletic career was difficult in many ways. People didn't want wheelchair racers competing in these events. There was booing, which made it extra difficult. But Deborah had a personal history with that kind of opposition. Deborah's bout with Guillain-Barré syndrome was quite severe. It was very tough on her, as her immune system attacked her nervous system, and for a while she was paralyzed from the neck down and needed a wheelchair.

When she was in college, certain people were opposed to her receiving a diploma because she couldn't write out her exams. She had to speak the answers. So, she fought for herself and got her diploma and eventually the disease abated, and she's had no real lasting effects. But she learned how to push back on unfairness, and when the time came, she did it for me. We have a special connection because, for a few years, my mom had a disability just like mine. She really does know how I feel in many situations. When people started to oppose my participation in athletic events, she got it immediately.

As you can see, they both have been instrumental in my success.

My parents have tons of skills. Bridget is the technology wizard. At work, she provided infrastructure support to the secretary of the U.S. Department of Health and Human Services while Debbie has run successful businesses, all focused on improving the lives of people with disabilities. At home, they were regular parents, sharing responsibilities for children who had unique challenges. Bridget helped me learn how to drive a car with hand controls while Debbie taught me how to "work a room." They took turns with doctor and school visits. They taught me how to cook and play cards and believe in myself. I tested their patience and, looking back, I am amazed at their resilience. I am full of love and respect for all they did to create meaningful lives for me and my sisters.

I'm in my early thirties now, and I believe all three McFadden girls are alike in all the ways that matter. We share an enthusiasm for life. A commitment to being our best. And a determination to make a difference. And all those qualities in us come from the example and upbringing we've had from our moms.

I am the luckiest girl in the world.

Photo Credit: Danny Meyer

STONE AND STEEL

Danny Meyer

Growing up, our family dynamic was pretty challenging. We had factions. My older sister was my mom's daughter. I was my dad's son. And my little brother was Switzerland.

These divisions appeared in various ways, but a clear one was politics. My mother's Chicago family were progressive and active Democrats. My dad's St. Louis family were—you guessed it—conservative and active Republicans. I came of age in the 1970s, and the Vietnam War and Watergate were part of many family discussions—notably at the dinner table.

My sister took my mother's side in these discussions, and I *wanted* to take my father's side. Yet I couldn't, because I didn't agree with him. Part of the reason was that my mom and I would watch Walter Cronkite every night. I was well-informed and sensed that my dad was wrong on these issues. This situation put a strain on an otherwise close relationship with my dad, and politics became a rare form of connection for me to my mom. Still, I didn't enjoy occupying the abyss between my parents.

In 1968, I was ten. I worked on a mock presidential campaign for Eugene McCarthy and handed out bumper stickers for a Democrat who won a seat in Congress for our district in St. Louis. To my dad's credit, he never gave me a hard time about it. We were paired up in our family's structure, yet he abided my political leanings despite how different they were from his own. It was part of our bond. After all, we did have St. Louis sports.

My mother, in those early years, abided little about me. Aside from politics, we were usually not on the same team. For one thing, she thought my brother and I were on the chubby side. She was concerned that we shopped for clothes in the "husky" aisle. She always told us to watch what we were eating, which only made us hungrier. I remember that Mom and her father got us a calorie-counting book, and my brother and I had to keep track of what we ate for about a year. Maybe that's why I have a somewhat unusual appreciation for watching other people enjoy food.

My mom was tough on me in other ways too. The most common refrain I heard from her was, "You're not living up to your potential." I knew what was going on. My sister, my mother's proxy in the family, was very highly achieving scholastically. I even heard it from one of my high school teachers: "Why aren't you as smart as your sister?"

My reaction was to back off and not give it my best. You can't lose if you're not playing. I said I was doing the best I could. But, of course, I was not bringing home distinguished grades of any kind. This approach only made my mom tougher. I heard her message all the time: "You're not living up to your potential." She was right about that.

My mother had another message for me too. She was always skeptical of social climbers and uber-achievers. She didn't trust people who sought popularity or status. When somebody would win an award or get any kind of recognition, she'd say, "That's a false measuring stick." I look back now and see that she was telling me there are many ways to be successful. She was trying to wake me up to the potential she saw in me but that remained out of my sight.

Things began to change a little as I approached college. Foolishly, I only applied to three schools, and none of them accepted me. My mother came into my room one day and said, fully exasperated, "You're going to the University of Chicago." She explained that her father, a trustee at the school, had arranged it. They were helping me, of course, but it felt like more of the same message: Danny can't get it done on his own, and we have to bail him out.

I told her I was not going to the University of Chicago. I wanted to make it on my own and then wrote the best letter of my life, which led to my being taken off the waitlist at Trinity College in Hartford, Connecticut. I finally woke up. I felt the fire in my belly and wanted to win. Fueled with a need to achieve, I pulled straight A's in my first semester at Trinity. From then on, I took things seriously. I bloomed and accepted the pressure of wanting to do well. I began to emerge from a nonproductive family dynamic, no longer in anyone's shadow. I was in it for myself. My years of underachieving were over.

They say it takes a stone to sharpen a blade. Without any question, my mother was that stone for me. It wasn't always fun when I was growing up. But she's the one who—more than anyone else—helped me see that I could be doing so much more.

While I was doing better personally, my parents' marriage continued to disintegrate, leading to their divorce. And I had outgrown my role of being my father's designated supporter in the family. I had become tired of having to prop up my dad so he could have an ally in his endless and needless war with my mom. He had been my protector for years, but that was no longer a legitimate reason to not have a relationship with my mom.

One day—following my junior year spring semester in Rome—I sat down with my mom and said, "We have to bury the hatchet." To my surprise, she was incredibly receptive. She broke down in tears and acknowledged what I said. She apologized for always holding me to a different standard than everyone else in the family. Mom couldn't believe that I was offering an olive branch to her. It was probably the best thing I've ever done.

But the cost was my relationship with my dad. He could handle that I was more liberal than he was, but he couldn't handle that I had closed the gap with my mom. It was devastating for me to lose his companionship. We had been very close all my life, almost more like friends than father and son. As much as it hurt to lose him, I never forgot that he had been asking me to make a choice that no son should ever have to face. He needed me to be "against" my mom, and I couldn't and didn't want to do it anymore.

After my parents divorced, things actually worked out okay for each of them. They each soon found a new spouse, and we no longer had to worry about one or the other being happy. And I enjoyed spending time with my mother's new husband. My dad passed away from cancer at fifty-nine, far too young an age, and sadly, too soon for the two of us to repair our relationship. After that conversation with my mom, she and I became very close and remained so until she died, just shy of her ninetieth birthday. She quickly showed how much she was now on my side. I had been planning to go to law school but bailed out at the last moment to pursue my passion for serving food. She encouraged me at every step of the way, adored our restaurants, and even invested in almost all of them.

Looking back, I can see that I wanted more than simply agreeing with my mom about President Nixon. I wanted her affection and approval too. I didn't see it for so many years. I also see now that a big part of my personality and set of gifts came from my mom. She was upbeat and positive and knows how to read and light up a room. She would have made a great maître d'.

I'm so glad that I was able to make this journey with my mom. And I am equally grateful for the times she pushed and pushed me to achieve more and to reach my potential. She gave me the gift of caring for other people and leaving things better than I found them. She taught me to be discerning in all things and especially to invest in quality relationships with quality people. There was a time early in my life when I was insecure and didn't necessarily look forward to tomorrow. But now, my attitude is that the best is yet to come. My mother gave that to me.

Photo Credit: Governor Wes Moore

SHE WORE SWEATERS SO WE COULD WEAR COATS

Governor Wes Moore

I sat down with Mom at the kitchen table as she scanned through my latest report card. This one looked the same as the last: I'd fallen to the bottom of my sixth-grade class after months of skipping school. One of my teachers suggested that I had a learning disability. My mother started to believe it might be true.

Then, one afternoon, my mom and I were riding in our family's Honda Civic when Chubb Rock came on the radio. I started singing along, word for word. My mother asked where I'd learned the lyrics. I explained that I heard the song for the very first time the day before. Mom pounced on the contradiction: I could memorize lyrics in a single afternoon but couldn't keep pace in English class. She turned and said, "Well, your grades obviously aren't bad because you can't pick this stuff up."

From that point on, my mom continued to challenge me to work harder in class. But she also advocated for me in front of school leaders, approaching my teachers and insisting that they try harder to reach me. She sat down with the same instructors who thought I had a learning disability and set them straight. "Wes isn't the problem. Your approach to him is the problem." My teachers wanted to label me and deflect responsibility. My mother refused to let that happen.

It took a while for me to realize my potential. But through the tireless support of my mother—her constant, unwavering belief that I could succeed inside and outside the classroom, no matter how others tried to place limits on my ability—I discovered my own power. I worked my way to the top of my class at Valley Forge Military Academy, earned a two-year college degree, graduated Phi Beta Kappa from Johns Hopkins University, and became a Rhodes scholar.

None of these achievements would have been possible without my mother's intervention back in the sixth grade. When I was falling behind, she demonstrated the values and vision that have defined her life: faith in others, commitment to family, and fearlessness in the face of authority. And Joy Thomas Moore, my mother, isn't just a courageous and powerful woman—she is also one of the most optimistic people I have ever known.

Her inner strength wasn't preordained; it was earned through years of trial and triumph, from her early childhood through adulthood. After I started to build a family of my own, my mother began to share with me the arc of her life as a daughter, sister, and mother. I've learned about the struggles she endured and the courage she brought to every obstacle. I believe her story offers a powerful lesson to all parents and guardians about resilience in the face of adversity. Because, while she suffered her share of heartaches, my mother has always preserved in an abiding belief that "joy cometh in the morning."

Joy Thomas Moore is the daughter of immigrants from Cuba and Jamaica. She grew up in the Jamaican parish of Trelawny and came to the United States when she was just a girl. At home, her family nurtured pride in the power of history and heritage. But on the playground, my mother's Caribbean roots quickly became a liability. Kids taunted her for speaking in a thick Jamaican dialect.

Even though she loved her homeland deeply, my mother spent hours in front of the radio studying the speech patterns of American disc jockeys and broadcasters so she could change her accent. With intense and intentional practice, her voice changed. Words like "constable" became "police officer." "Irie" became "cool." Instead of being defeated by the name-callers and bullies, she rose above their slights. My mother learned to adapt to a new country, a new world, and a new language on her own. Even at a young age, she lived with tenacity and dedication, and her resilience would come to define every chapter of her life.

If "fitting in" marked the first big test of my mother's journey, then "moving out" marked the second. She attended American University and started dating a charismatic undergraduate named Bill. They soon got married. But as time went on, Bill became increasingly dependent on drugs and alcohol. He grew demanding and volatile around his family, taking out aggression on those closest to him.

My mother was young, still finding her footing, and had just given birth to my older sister, Nikki. Bill offered financial support and a measure of security to both of them. But money couldn't redeem his abuse. After only a brief period of marriage, my mother packed up Nikki's things, and they left in the middle of the night. Joy divorced Bill and never looked back. Given the choice between stability and respect, my mother chose respect.

Still, my mother's greatest test was yet to come. After leaving Bill, she found the love of her life and remarried. My mom and my dad had two children: me and my younger sister, Shani. A few years later, my father became sick with a rare but curable disease. But his condition went unrecognized and untreated by doctors. He died in front of me before my fourth birthday. In an instant, my mother became a single mom of three. She had to grieve an unimaginable loss while keeping our family afloat. Yet, despite the challenges, nothing could destroy her hope.

She gave me, Shani, and Nikki a wonderful childhood—and cared for us in the best way imaginable. She buried her pain and disappointment because she knew she had to devote herself to raising three kids who counted on her leadership as the head of the household. Shani once said, "Mom wore sweaters so we could wear coats." And it's true. She sacrificed for us, no matter what was required. Her love for us was limitless.

My mother attended every sports game, listened to every heartbreak, and encouraged every dream—especially if it challenged the mold of what was to be expected or if others doubted her confidence. After I felt handcuffs on my wrists at eleven years old, many people around me started to distance themselves from my life and my story. But my mother went out of her way to introduce me to mentors who helped bend my trajectory toward success. And when I decided to join the United States Army at seventeen, my mother had the courage to support my decision, even though most members of our family considered it a bad idea. She was—and still is—my guardian, my protector, and my champion.

I stand in awe of my mother every single day. By the time I was a teenager, she had endured bullying, tragedy, and financial strain. Still, she always remained composed, compassionate, and confident before the world. We never saw her flinch.

As I've grown older, I've tried to understand the source of that iron will. How could she keep going, even after enduring the worst? What kept her optimism alive, even after coming face-to-face with so much darkness?

One force that helps my mother keep her faith in the future is her knowledge of the past. I've experienced the power of this mindset firsthand. One of the ways she nurtured a spirit of optimism within me and my sisters was to stress the importance of history, whether it be family history, U.S. history, or the history of Black struggle in America. She has often reminded me that we are only here because of people who marched and prayed over generations: people who may not have known us, but who still believed in the hope of us. If they could persevere, so can we.

When you acknowledge all those who brought you to this point, you can't help but push toward the horizon. If there was anybody who had the right to harbor hate, frustration, and disappointment, it was my mom. But she refused to be defined by the worst moments of her life—and kept on searching for the good. She understood from a young age that her ability to succeed wasn't freely given; it was hard-won by all those who came before. That's the fuel that kept her going. And as a mother, she instilled that same philosophy in every member of our family.

My work in the Maryland State House isn't easy. But whenever a challenge feels insurmountable, I remember the creed my mother taught me, and I put my immediate surroundings into a broader perspective. Our history is our power, and our past teaches us that any obstacle can be overcome, every problem can be solved, and no hardship is permanent. This is part of the mindset that propelled my mother forward. And now, as a father myself, I try to mirror those values for my son and daughter—James and Mia.

One of the best things any parent can do is remind their loved ones that we stand on the shoulders of giants. I stand on my mother's shoulders. My mother stands on her parents' shoulders and her friends' shoulders. And I want my two children to not only recognize the shoulders they stand on—but also to understand that someday, there will be others who stand on their shoulders too. I believe that recognizing your place in a long legacy of fighters and dreamers is one of the most important ways we can keep the faith and preserve that optimism my mother still embodies to this day.

The work I describe isn't easy: It requires constant focus and small acts of remembrance. But every so often, the power of history presents itself in vivid detail. On the morning of my inauguration as Maryland's sixty-third governor, I asked a group of a few hundred people to join me at the Annapolis City Dock to honor the enslaved men and women who had been taken through that port against their will. We held a wreath-laying ceremony and marched from the docks to the State House, a place built by enslaved people. My wife and I brought Mia and James down to the docks with us that morning to make sure they understood the history that brought our family to that particular moment. I'd like to think that experience reached their hearts.

I also make sure that I'm there for my kids as they make history of their own. One lasting lesson I received from my mother was to be present, whether that means being home for dinner every night or driving two hours to a basketball game. We only get so many years in which we can truly "be there" for our children as they write new chapters in their own stories. Mia has discovered a passion for dance over the last few years, and there's nothing I love more than getting to see her perform. James has taken after his dad and started getting into sports. Even after a long week of work, I relish the chance to watch him play flag football with friends.

In a tribute to the importance of being there for each other and celebrating the legacies we build, no matter age or background, I have a standing rule: My children are welcome to show up for anything that I do in my life, especially in my work. If they're curious about a certain issue or topic, they can always sit in on a meeting or attend an event that links back to their interests. They are not required to do anything other than observe and learn—but they always have an open invitation. I want them to know what their dad is up to—and get a sense of our family's story as it's being written.

This rule is one of the ways I try to be present for my kids—to let them know they are my priority and that I welcome finding ways for us to be together. But more than that, I hope these experiences will help teach them that the world is much larger than what is directly in front of them. My mother knew that, and she made a point of using that knowledge to lead her toward a deeper, more lasting optimism. As a parent, I yearn to hand down that same wisdom to my children.

Joy isn't something we discover from within; it's a tradition we inherit. I hope that tradition lives on for generations to come—and through our common efforts, I believe it will.

Photo Credit: Kevin Nealon

BE AVAILABLE

Kevin Nealon

ooking back on my childhood, my main sense of my mother, Kathleen Kimball Nealon, is that she was always there for us, always taking care of the family. She did our laundry, laid our clothes out for us every night, and did the cooking—which she was really good at. We had a delicious dinner every night at six o'clock, when my dad got home from work. In the morning, there were eggs, bacon, pancakes…pretty much whatever you might find on an IHOP menu.

We had the best brown paper bag lunches. Mom would make scrumptious egg salad or tuna salad on fresh bread. She also accommodated me with my unusual request: a baked bean sandwich (not on the IHOP menu), which—to avoid ridicule—I would tell my classmates was chunky peanut butter. Now, mind you, she didn't carry the load of work all by herself. My brothers, sisters, and I all also chipped in. We were the ones who had to wear the clothes she washed, we were the ones who had to digest the dinners and desserts she made, and we were the ones who had to carry those brown paper bag lunches all the way to school!

Mom also entertained a lot, hosting dinner parties with my dad or joining him in the social aspect of his work. She was also very supportive of my father while he pursued his career as an aeronautical engineer at Sikorsky Aircraft in Connecticut. They were a great team and a fun couple because they both had a great sense of humor. I remember an occasion when I picked her up at the train station. I pulled up to the front and yelled to her through my opened car window, "Hey, lady? You want a ride?" The nearby, concerned people implored her not to take this stranger up on his offer. She smiled slightly and went along with my little joke. She walked down the steps, climbed into the car, and off we went, laughing hilariously.

Her calm approach to life has also stayed with me. I would ask my mom, "How did you take care of all of us? How did you divide your attention amongst us?" She said she would just tend to whoever was having problems. That sums her up in a way, that kind of straightforward, simple approach to raising five children.

You may think I am making up all these wonderful traits in her because perhaps I was actually a latchkey kid with an absent, uncaring mother. Maybe I have created the mother I wish I did have. First of all, thank you for thinking I am that creative, but I am not rewriting history. Now you might think she spoiled us; the truth is, we never came to expect or demand her generosity and love, although we were all very grateful.

Here is another instance of me not creating a false scenario for my psychological well-being. Before my mother married my father, she worked as a secretary for a general at the Pentagon. She became extremely adept at typing. Since I couldn't type, she offered her services to type my term papers. I'd hear her late into the night—tap tap tap. In the mornings, I would hear the squeaky ironing board as she ironed our school clothes. Honestly, how were we supposed to fall asleep with all that tapping? How were we supposed to sleep in with all that squeaking of the ironing board?

She wasn't a helicopter mother, yet she was always aware of what we were doing. And she wasn't a worrywart. She gave us the leeway to do what we wanted to do, but there were sensible limits. I was told many times not to ride on a minibike or a motorcycle. My mom considered them death traps. Well, one day, going against her wishes, I rode on the back of a friend's minibike. He took a corner rather sharply and, concerned we would fall, I put my foot down and sprained my ankle. I hobbled home expecting the worst, but instead she consoled me and iced my ankle. She didn't need to read me the riot act, because she knew I had learned my lesson. I have never ridden a minibike or motorcycle since that day.

Mom taught me not to dwell too much on disappointments. She'd say, "Okay, all right. That happened. We survived, so let's move on." She always encouraged us to not obsess over little things. When I think about it, moving on was a big part of my mom's approach to life.

Often, on a weekday morning, I wouldn't want to get out of bed. I would try to convince my mother that I was feeling slightly under the weather and probably shouldn't go to school. Upbeat, she would throw open the drapes and say, "You just need a little sunshine. Let's get the day going." She would know the difference between my actually being sick and my just not wanting to go to school.

All I ever really wanted to be was a comedian. By the time I was fifteen or sixteen, I was memorizing jokes and telling them at parties. Friends encouraged me to look into those comedy clubs in New York City, only a ninety-minute trek from my house (not on a minibike or motorcycle). I eventually did look into those clubs, but New York was not the right atmosphere for me. So, I headed to California. My mother probably didn't want me to move away, but she was totally supportive. She was concerned for how it would work out for me, but she also wanted me to follow my passion, for which I am forever grateful.

I learned one thing above all from my mother's parenting style: Be available. Be present in my son's life. I've made a priority of spending time with him because of the example my mother lived. I will not, however, stay up late at night typing his term paper or ironing his clothes!

Summing up my mom is not easy because she stood for so many wonderful things. I can't overstate how special she was. It was as though she was put together, piece by piece, to be the perfect mother. But a standout quality of my mother's was how caring she was. Even very late in her life, she did not want us to worry about her. When time was catching up to her, she became dependent on a cane. We knew her leg was not likely to become strong again, but she would say, "You know this cane is only temporary. I'll be fine."

We all knew it wasn't temporary, but we went along with it, as she undoubtedly did for me many times along the way. Thank you, Mom. I love you.

Photo Credit: Soledad O'Brien

MOST PEOPLE ARE IDIOTS

Soledad O'Brien

My mother, Estela Marquetti y Mendieta O'Brien, was one of those people who really believed that you could achieve whatever you put your mind to.

She grew up in Cuba, and her family was very, very poor. It was clear that only one of the five children would have a chance at an education. But Mom was curious, bright, and determined from a very young age. So her parents decided that she was the one who would go to school, learn English, move to America, get married, and have a chance at a better life.

That decision by her parents changed her life for the better, to say the least, though it also gave her an acute case of survivor's guilt. She got the opportunity, and she could not waste it. And she didn't. As a result, my life has had a completely different trajectory than that of my Cuban cousins, just as my mother's life was so different from those of her siblings.

My mother studied English through the Havana chapter of the Oblate Sisters of Providence, a religious institute based in Baltimore that was founded for the education of girls of African descent.

In 1944, the Sisters arranged for my fourteen-year-old mother to leave Cuba and come to the United States. At the time, you could go back and forth quite easily. She was steadily establishing herself in this country and, while living with the Oblate Sisters in Baltimore, went to a local high school and then attended Notre Dame of Maryland University, one of the few colleges in the country at that time that accepted Black women.

She met my father when she got a job in the chemistry department at Johns Hopkins University, where my dad, who was from Australia, was getting his PhD. They met because they both went to daily Mass, and he would always offer her a ride. At first, she regularly turned it down because it was not appropriate. Eventually, she relented, and they went on a date. They married in 1958.

It started to get harder to go back and forth as Fidel Castro rose to power. My mother eventually decided not to go back to Cuba in 1959, and the result of her parents' choice to give her a way out of Cuba took a dramatic turn. She essentially said goodbye to her past, and the pressure to make it work in America grew even more. Her drive was innate, but it was intensified by the way her life played out. She set goals for herself and her family, and she was going to make sure the chance her family took on her would pay off for everybody.

My father eventually got a job at State University of New York at Stony Brook, so my parents moved their family to Long Island.

My parents were a biracial couple at a time when it wasn't widely accepted. But that never stopped them from having the life they wanted. There were customs and covenants at the time that said Black people had to leave certain towns at sunset unless they were working. My parents didn't care, but they had a hard time finding people who were willing to sell them a house. Eventually, they found a guy who parceled off three acres of his land in St. James and sold them to my dad, and that's where they built our house.

By 1967, my parents had six children, ranging from one to seven years old. My mom was not the kind of mom who sat on the floor and played with her kids. She saw her role as homemaker, to make sure the kids and house were clean, to prepare dinner every night, and to see to it that everything was together and well organized. It had to run like clockwork, and it did, with no help. Her plan was that her children would make the most of their lives, and her part was to provide a strong foundation and emphasize education and hard work.

Both of my parents, as immigrants, believed that the great thing about America was that you can be anything you put your mind to, and my parents saw their job as helping us figure out what we wanted to be. In this sense, they were ambitious for us.

After all, my mother had left her own country, learned a new language, got an education, and started a family by the time she was thirty. Now, she put that energy to work for us. Her story has always inspired me and my siblings to work hard to not let anyone or anything stop us on the way to our dreams.

A big part of my mother's philosophy was education. She taught us that your education is something that can't be taken from you at the border or at a crossroad in your life. She valued education and showed us that with the right education or training, you can put your head down and get things done.

My mother's focus was an important part of my childhood. We were pretty much the only Black kids in our schools growing up. And the Ku Klux Klan had been active in the area in the 1920s; members of the Klan were buried in the cemetery across from the library. But the town had good schools, so the idea was to assimilate. Put your head down, fit in, and get a good education. Stick to the plan. Nothing matters except what we're going to get out of this situation.

She once told me that it didn't matter that no one wanted to date me. That wasn't what we were trying to accomplish; there was a strategy in place, and we had other goals. "You'll meet more people in college," she told me. She was no fool, and she was strategic about everything.

I do not mean to imply that my mother was not loving. She would give her arm for one of her kids. She was loving in that way. I think a lot of immigrant moms are like that. They don't coddle and snuggle you. But if you were sick, she would clean everything up, strip down your bed, put on perfectly clean sheets, and you could sleep in peace in a tightly made bed. That's how she showed her love. She didn't pamper you, but she was looking out for you.

Part of my mother's approach also involved being prepared. She took things as they came along and dealt with them. We had a big family with a lot going on, but it never felt chaotic, and she pulled this off while holding down a full-time teaching job.

My mother was also very wise about race, and she was very direct when talking about it. She said two things that I think were so smart and helpful. She used to say to us, "Don't let anybody tell you you're not Black. Don't let anybody say you're not Latina."

My thought was, *Hey, lady! We're in an all-white neighborhood. Where are people talking like that? Nobody says things like that to us.* Later on, I realized how much confidence that idea gave me. I went into the world very clear on who I was.

I remember the first time those particular words of hers made sense to me. I was working on a series of documentaries at CNN called *Black in America*. I dealt with people wondering if I was Black enough. And it hit me. "This is what my mom was talking about." Her words guided me through those moments, all those years later.

Another wonderful thing she said to us was, "I love your father most of all, and then I love all the rest of you equally." I've come to see that my mother's message was a good and powerful one: You build your life and family on the foundation of a strong relationship. And that allows you to love all your children equally. My mom was always so didactic and so clear with her lessons for us.

My mom could be a stubborn pain in the ass, and I can be one too. Toughness was a big part of her makeup. She would throw a complete hissy fit if you didn't make your bed. Yet, I remember calling her from an ambulance after tearing up my knee playing rugby in college. She said, "Okay, I'll let you talk to your father." She didn't want to talk about her child getting injured. She cared, of course, but wasn't going to baby me over it. Dad can handle that one. But God forbid you didn't make your bed. She wanted to talk about that! All hell would break loose. That was very classic of my mom. She would go nutty over little things. But big things? It's not a problem. Absolutely solvable.

I also take after my mom when it comes to strategy and preparation. When I talk to young journalists, I tell them I timed my pregnancies very intentionally around contracts, because it's not fun to negotiate in "TV land" while pregnant. People don't like it, even if they tell you they do— they don't. And you lose money. I often find women are getting bad advice on this topic. *You should talk to someone in management.* I say, *Tell no one.*

I think you have to be strategic and plan your career and life moves carefully. I think years ahead when it comes to work and where I want to live in ten years. I've already planned it out, and I learned that from my mom.

My mother also had a saying that is a little controversial, though I think it's kind of funny. The message is strong and wise, and I've seen undeniably that it is also true. My mother often said to me, "People are idiots and, if you are listening to them, you might be an idiot too."

Whenever I would bring my troubles to my mom and I would say, "Everybody says I won't get the job," or "Everybody says I can't do it," she would immediately say, "What do they know? People are idiots."

She'd go on to say that people don't know what you can do. They might be afraid to do what you are trying to do. These people aren't even doing what you want to do. So, why listen to them?

Over time, I think her words, however blunt, have proven to be true. It's best to believe in yourself and not be swayed by what other people think or say to you. Her use of a phrase like that is partially due to a slight language barrier; she spoke perfectly good English but perhaps lacked the vocabulary required for nuance in certain situations. But she was also very direct in the way she spoke. She got to the point.

What I also learned from my mother with that observation was to be skeptical of negative people or negative feedback. My mother taught me to see through it immediately and push it away. She also helped me to realize how rarely you speak to an expert. You're usually hearing from random people. She taught me how to tune out people who just like to weigh in. The people wondering if I am Black enough. Or the people telling you to share your pregnancy news with your manager. You know, idiots.

My mother's words also come from personal experience. My parents got married at a time when biracial marriage was widely frowned upon and even illegal in some places. But they did it anyway. She had personal experience of doing what she wanted, what she felt was right, and not listening to naysayers. People told them not to have kids because biracial kids would have trouble fitting in. They did what they wanted. They both were very good at living the idea of "What do you want to do? Figure it out and go do it."

One of my most cherished stories about my mother and what I learned from her involves many of her best qualities. My mother drove a gold Chevrolet Chevette, and she drove it very slowly and would stubbornly not react to other drivers honking or yelling at her. It was so funny, too, because she would swear at the other drivers in her somewhat idiosyncratic English, using word combinations that did not exist, and I'd be there correcting how my mother swore.

When I came home from college during freshman year, my mother would let me drive her Chevette if I dropped her off at school and picked her up at the end of the school day. One day, I went to school to take her home, and I wanted to use the car afterwards. As my mother and I were leaving the school, we came upon a scene that unfolded in a way that has stayed with me.

My mother and I saw that the principal and vice principal had stopped a young Black kid who was about fourteen years old. It's important to remember that we didn't have a lot of Black kids at our school. Picture my mother walking into this moment. She's wearing a hat with a skunk-like purple stripe down it, and she had her PBS tote bag. When we got close to them, my mother stopped. The two white men said, "Hi, Mrs. O'Brien. You can move along. We're handling this." The Black kid looked at my Black mom, and they connected silently.

"No, I'm good," said my mother, and she then just stood there. As I said, my mother could be a pain in the ass. No one bossed her around, even these two men who were essentially her bosses.

I'm thinking, *I want to keep moving and get her home so I can use the car.* It started to get weird. I said, "Come on, Mom." She said, again, "I'm good."

This young Black kid is watching, and he's witnessing things change a bit. To be clear, he wasn't in danger; they were maybe bullying him slightly because he was young and didn't go to our school. Still, my mom refused to move.

"We have this under control, Mrs. O'Brien."

"It's okay. I'm good," she said, now looking at the young boy. I remember him looking at my mom and being so relieved. Her look told him, "I'm not leaving. Whatever this is, I'm staying."

I was blown away by the scene. It was so funny to me to see my mom, all five feet two inches of her, in her skunk hat with her PBS tote bag, completely ignoring the obvious power vacuum in that encounter. Soon, it all got awkward and embarrassing, even for the principal, who could fire my mom. Finally, he turned to the kid and said, "Remember, there's no running in the halls." And they let him go on his way. As soon as the boy and the principals left, my mom said, "Okay. We can leave."

That story is a clear example of something both my parents were good at, especially my mom. She saw the importance of witnessing things and not letting people go through tough moments alone. Even though, in this story, she really had no power, other than her personal strength and integrity.

She showed me that you can sometimes just stay where you are and be a witness. Watch things unfold. Without speaking, she let that kid know she wasn't going anywhere. And she did it by saying and doing very little. She didn't move closer to them. She didn't raise her voice or move a limb. It was very cool for me to see my mom go from being somewhat annoying by not moving away to becoming the center of power in that brief scene. Her fearlessness, her unwillingness to kowtow to anyone, has stayed with me and guided me.

It's funny. We never talked about it. Years later, I told her how cool she was that day. All she said was, "Well, those people could be bullies." She was the living embodiment of understanding the value of standing up for people who can't stand up for themselves. That boy had no capacity to resist those men. And she did it at some personal risk, for a child she never saw before and would never see again, even if it was just upsetting some important relationships at the school.

As a journalist, I've seen that there is tremendous power in simply not moving when you're sent on your way. You may not be able to do anything, but you can stand there, take notes, roll your camera, and witness it. Then you can say, "I was there. Here's what happened."

My mother also influenced the way I approach life when she would remind me that we all get the same twenty-four hours. It's up to us to decide how we spend them. When I would complain about not having enough time, my mother would remind me that my day is up to me. It caused me to think, eventually, about what I say "yes" to and what I say "no" to. It was a lesson in prioritizing things in my life and has proven a valuable way to look at my day and my life.

She had another variation on this twenty-four-hour theme. My mother was a big believer in limiting your wallowing in disappointment over things that don't go your way or things that work out differently than you expected. She said take twenty-four hours, sit in bed, cry, and eat Häagen-Dazs. Have your moment of sadness or self-pity. But at hour twenty-five, you start making lists, pros and cons or whatever, and building your plan to respond.

And today, I'm exactly that person. As a reporter, you have to be flexible and nimble as you pursue a story. You start with a plan, and you might see that it's not working out. So, let's try plan B. Okay, that's not working either. Let's move on to plan C. You don't have time to feel sorry for yourself. You have to keep working and working and working until you get what you want. That attitude has really stuck with me. I'm a big list maker. I live my life on lists and being prepared.

My mother lived through a very different time. My mother lived in an era where you waited to see if you could do something, if you'd get approval. Can my kid go to this class? Can we live in this neighborhood? Can I marry this person? My parents made their way in America by deciding that they were going to figure out what they wanted to do and then go and do it. They weren't going to internalize other people's feedback about what kind of lives they should or could live. They weren't going to be told what they could or could not do. Because if they had, I promise you I certainly wouldn't be here.

Photo Credit: Ms. Rachel

IMAGINE SOMETHING BETTER AND MAKE IT REAL

Ms. Rachel

My mom built me and my sister a treehouse. Singlehandedly. She imagined it, and then she built it—all while raising us as a single mom.

Even today when I ask my mom how she knew how to build a treehouse, she shrugs it off and says she's just interested in how things come together. Back then there was no internet, so you couldn't google "how to build a treehouse" or follow a YouTube tutorial. Somehow, she built it, nail by nail, board by board, until we had what was the most epic treehouse ever. We would climb up the long rope ladder, wave out the windows, and talk about dreams of our own on the balcony.

Susannah believed she could do it ,and she did. She's just a firecracker of a person and she can't be stopped… all five feet one of her. Couch needed to be moved up a flight of stairs? She'd do it. Pipes needed to be fixed? She'd do it. Were some of these things ill-advised? Probably. Occasionally we'd hear her shout something like "I have the dresser moved halfway up the stairs, and I'm underneath it. Come quick!"

She paired that determination with imagination, always seeing potential to make something more fun, more alive. When we had a school performance dancing around to a song about red sneakers, she could have sent us to school in red shirts. Instead, she made us red sneaker costumes out of boxes that had the audience in giggles. Some people would have seen boxes. She saw rad red sneaker costumes.

She also taught me that what you imagine doesn't have to fit someone else's mold. My mom is now sixty-seven, and she still does cartwheels. "I want to be able to do a cartwheel in my nineties," she says. When we were kids, my mom would jump on the couch and sing Carole King songs or songs from musicals with us. One time she brought us to the beach at night, and we danced around with sparklers and climbed on rocks. That night is a core memory for me. Her joyful spirit and boundless energy have always inspired me. She's also AWTBS, which is an acronym I just made up: **A**lways **w**illing **to** **b**e **s**illy. I inherited that one.

She emphasized to my sister and me that Mister Rogers was right: We were both wonderful the way we were. Going through school, I followed my older sister, Rebecca, who was so smart in every subject and effortlessly aced every test. Academia didn't come as easily to me. I thought, *Did the teachers who had her first expect me to be as smart and feel disappointed?*

Rebecca was in the gifted and talented program, and I hoped I could be in it too!

When I was nominated to try out for it, I was thrilled. I took a test to get in that probably had a bunch of logical and memory-based puzzles and problems, which I'm not great at. Then, one night my mom came in my room and told me I hadn't been accepted into the program. I started bawling. I thought, *I guess I'm not smart enough*. She told me I was brilliant in a different way, and she knew I'd do great things with the unique gifts and talents I had. Her approach was like the saying, "Everyone is a genius. But if you judge a fish by its ability to climb a tree, it will live its whole life thinking it is stupid."

The idea that you could imagine something better and make it real helped me become Ms. Rachel. When my son began to have challenges with speech, I looked for a show that encouraged language development and milestones. He's a visual learner and learned well from video. When I couldn't find the show I was looking for, I realized I should try to make it! (With the help of my amazing husband, Aron!) I balanced a camera on a stack of books, and I just started creating. Seven years and 119 videos later, I'm so overjoyed hearing from little ones and their families all over the world whose kids are learning and growing along with our videos.

My mother's imagination didn't stop with bringing these sparks of joy and creativity to our lives. She imagined a better world, where everyone was loved and had what they needed. She found endless ways to make that happen too. She organized a neighborhood yard sale for people in need where all the items were free. She went back to college to finish her degree and then to get a master's while waiting tables, working at a daycare, and caring for two daughters so she could become a social worker. She volunteered with local organizations. She went above and beyond for families she worked with who were struggling. My mom even wrote a letter to Mother Teresa about her desire to help the poor. Mother Teresa wrote back to thank her for her efforts and dedication to the poor.

Another lesson learned from my mother is unconditional love. I remember one time when I was younger, she and I got into an argument, and I went to bed feeling a little sad. But when I woke up, she had made this mobile with the various parts listing the kind, sweet, joyous traits she said I had. It was hanging from the light in the living room. She had stayed up all night making it, and it was one of the most beautiful mobiles I've ever seen.

She taught us that we are all connected. It's because of what she taught us, and more importantly what she modeled for us, that I feel a responsibility to use my voice to advocate for a better world for each and every child. I advocate for investment in early childhood, which is essential to help all children have the chance to meet their full potential. I couldn't stay silent when I saw the unimaginable suffering of children in Gaza. My mom taught us the Golden Rule and to love every neighbor, no exceptions.

I never thought I'd be so well known for YouTube. I never thought I'd wrap my arms around an adorable girl who's lost her legs in an airstrike, laughing together as we sing her favorite song. I wouldn't be doing these things without my mom showing me that I could imagine better for myself, my kids, and for everyone.

Photo Credit: Robin Roberts

THERE IS NO LIMIT ON GRATITUDE

Robin Roberts

My father, Lawrence Roberts, served with the Tuskegee Airmen in World War II and ended up spending thirty-five years in the military, retiring from the Air Force as a colonel. My mother, Lucimarian Tolliver Roberts, told me that they moved twenty-three times during his career.

I'm the youngest, so by the time I came along, the moving around had slowed considerably. But it was a big influence on me to watch how they treated each other. It was nothing they ever said but rather what they did. It was an incredible partnership. And I think it was also part of a plan my mother had for herself.

My parents met at Howard University in Washington, DC. They were both the first people in their families to attend college. There is an old joke that kind of applies to my mother in that she didn't go to college to get a BS but rather an MRS degree. She found my dad, and they built a wonderful life and family together.

Mom was a loving and supportive wife, and she made sure that all twenty-three of those military houses were truly our *homes*. She knew her role in the partnership was to handle the home front.

She used her creativity to make a caring home and family environment. For instance, we always ate dinner by candlelight. I loved it as a kid, and we'd all want to be the one who lit the candles or blew them out. I assumed everyone ate like that, and I was surprised when I went to someone else's house and they didn't light candles when we ate. Mama told me she did that because the houses in the military were so dreary. Mama said everything looked better in candlelight, so that's what she did.

Had she been born in a different time, my mother's life may have looked more like mine. She would have definitely had a career instead of short stints as a teacher or real estate agent and other jobs along the way. It didn't bother her that my father's career came first in the family, but once he retired and went into private business, it became her turn. She flourished immediately, joining boards and supporting causes that mattered to her.

At this time in her life, Mom showed me that, as she used to say, "You can have it all, just not all at the same time." She waited until I graduated from high school, and she knew it was her time to fly, and she just took off.

My mother told me that around this time, she was in the bathtub, and she looked up and said, "Lord, I know that you have more that you want me to do." In a way, you could say that she really did get a call at that time.

She had always been active in politics and in the community. She was well known in Biloxi, Mississippi, where my parents had chosen to stay after my father retired. She was on the Democratic Women's Committee, and the next thing you know she got a call from the governor asking her to be on the State Board of Education in Mississippi. Eventually, she became the first Black person to chair that board.

Then she was appointed to the Mississippi Coast Coliseum Commission, a board that oversees the local coliseum and convention center. She ended up the president of that group too. As you can see, my mother was the kind of person who would be appointed to a committee and end up as the chairperson. She was director of the Federal Reserve Bank of Atlanta, New Orleans branch too. She didn't accept these positions until I was off to college, and it was nice to see that my dad was more than happy to tag along, now as the spouse. Things had changed.

It was wonderful to see my mother have her time. She had simply put her dreams on hold, and we were very happy for her to finally have the spotlight.

Along the way, my mother taught me how to treat people. She listened to people, and she always made people feel valued and seen and heard. She knew the name of the person who owned the building and the name of the custodian. She used to say that she never knew any strangers, just friends she hadn't met yet. And she lived that idea to its fullest.

When I was helping her write her memoir, we were working on the acknowledgments. The list was extremely long, and, as a journalist, I was trying to edit down to essentials. I said something about it. She sat back in her chair, pushed her glasses up on her nose, and said, "Child, you can't put a limit on gratitude."

Along the same lines, my mom always told me that you never know who's watching. You never know the impact that you can have on somebody. It's very hard to make it on your own in this world, so it's best to make a habit of being pleasant every day and to not only be grateful but also to acknowledge the people who played any part in your success.

My mother also had a toughness and courage that showed me a lot. It was difficult for us to be the only Black family around. My father was a high-ranking officer, but there weren't a lot of other Black men in similar roles. Early on in my father's career, my mother was denied entry into the officers' wives club at Keesler Air Force Base in Biloxi. Years later, when we were stationed back in Biloxi, Mom became—surprise—the president of the officers' wives club.

She was very clear on who she was and who she wanted her children to be. Over time, I learned so much from her courage, clarity, and confidence.

During one career day when I was in junior high school, I went from station to station in the gym and learned about various professions from people who were in those fields. I was very much into sports, and I wanted to find a way to have a career in sports. But there were very few avenues for women into sports.

I came home from career day and told my mom that I wanted to be a physical education teacher and a coach because that's what was available for women when it came to sports. My mom said, "No. Keep looking. That can't be the only thing you think you can do."

I thought she'd be happy, because she'd proudly been a teacher herself. But she was telling me not to be limited by what people say and try to fit into a certain role. She wasn't forcing me to do anything but rather encouraging me to be responsible for my choices and to be thorough in my evaluation of what was possible. She showed me the wisdom of taking time for things to become clear to me, to slow down a bit when it came to big decisions.

It always touched me that she took the time to get to know her children as individuals. She knew who we were and helped us to see things in ourselves and, maybe, what our dreams should be. I am very grateful for that, and I have drawn on it daily over the years.

Because I studied journalism in college, my sister Sally-Ann suggested that I combine my interest in journalism with my love of sports. It was such a great idea, and I knew it was right for me. My dad was very military, and he felt I should go into hard news because that's where I'd make the most money.

But my mother told me to follow my heart. So, I took part-time positions in sports for far less money than I could have made in news at the time. And I was never happier than when I was doing that. I eventually made the transition from sports to news based on something else my mother taught me. She told me to not be afraid to venture outside my comfort zone. I was comfortable in sports, and

I had been saying no to news opportunities out of habit. I'd been saying no so long that I didn't really mean it any longer. My mother was always a great sounding board.

She could be practical too. One time when I was at ESPN, they offered me a contract that I didn't think was good enough. I felt my hard work and commitment had earned a better salary and told my mother I would rather flip burgers than sign this contract. She said, "I've flipped burgers. Sign the contract."

Another time I thought I didn't get a job because I was a Black woman. This was early in my career, right out of college, and I thought it was a case of discrimination.

My mom listened to me and then said, "Well, honey, maybe you didn't get it because you're not good enough yet."

When your mom says something like that to you, it makes you think. I realized she was telling me to not let anyone, or myself, make me think that any outcome is because of my gender or race or anything like that. Both of my parents were very firm about that. Don't give the enemy any more ammunition. You might not be the best in every situation, but you should always strive to be the best you can be. They really instilled that in me.

Still, my mother was not blind to the realities of race in this country. I remember one time my sisters and I were giving her a hard time because we thought she was coddling and showing favoritism to our brother.

She sat us down pretty quickly. She said, "Now listen, girls. You have no idea what it's like to be a Black man in this country." She paused. "So, yes, I'm guilty of showing your brother a little favoritism, because I know how hard it is for him out there."

She was telling us so much in that conversation, things she had learned in her own life by watching, and paying attention to, the lives of her father, husband, and son. No parent wants to be seen as favoring one child over the others, but when she explained it to us, we understood immediately. She wasn't downplaying any racism we might face but was reminding us of our brother's journey and what she knew he had to confront on a regular basis.

My mother was also always reminding me to believe in myself. One time, I was at a crossroads about my career at ESPN. Mom said, "Robin, that's because you think that the only opportunities available to you are in sports. That's your thinking. But that's not who you are."

Soon after, I attended a party in New York in the neighboring apartment building. It was an impressive gathering. Oprah Winfrey was there, as well as other luminaries. I saw that I could hold a conversation with them, and they wanted to hear what I had to say. I was taking it all in on my way home.

I called my mom and just said, "Thank you."

Photo Credit: Al Roker

SHE LOVED FIERCELY

Al Roker

Everything I know about my mom is from my childhood on.

She didn't talk a lot about her upbringing. We heard about her siblings, my uncle Charlie and aunt Monica, but not a lot about their younger days. I know she grew up in a big house, big enough for a couple of her sisters to eventually live there with their families.

I don't think she had a difficult upbringing. She didn't talk about it. She was a very pragmatic, no-nonsense kind of woman. If she had hard times, she probably just brushed them aside and kept moving forward.

I knew her parents, and she didn't particularly take after either one of them. Pop was strict, but he wasn't mean. He was a kind, gentle guy. My grandmother was a quiet woman, but she expressed herself. She saw my future too. She often said, "The way he talks, he could be on TV." She didn't live to see it, but she was onto something.

It's funny to think about it this way, but I have a hard time separating my parents in my mind. I don't even have many individual pictures of them. They were joined at the hip and a great couple, true soulmates. I put them both on a pedestal, and being their son is one of the great blessings I've had in this life. Al and Izzy. Izzy and Al. I saw them as one unit.

My mother, Isabel, was a tough but loving parent.

She was also a very honest woman. My daughter Leila takes after her. I remember when we were looking at elementary schools for her. She interviewed at one all-girls school that prides itself on raising strong young women. The headmaster told us that Leila was a little blunt! At five years old she was, maybe, a little *too* strong for them. But isn't that what you want?

One time my wife, Deborah Roberts, came to me and said I needed to have a word with my mom. Deborah said Mom was playing games with the kids and not letting them win. That's my mom.

Later, we had some friends over to the house, adults, and they were playing Monopoly with Leila, and she was cleaning their clocks. One of the adults said, "Well, somebody sure taught you how to play Monopoly."

And Leila said, "My nana."

Deborah did speak to my mom about it, but Mom was unapologetic about her approach. She wasn't going to let them win. She said, "That is not the way they learn." She wanted to teach them how to play the game and become good at it.

It was the same way when I was growing up. We played Boggle, Monopoly, and Trouble, the game with the "Pop-O-Matic" that rolled the dice for you.

Mom used an egg timer when we played Scrabble. You didn't have all day to make your move. She was, in her way, exacting. There is a correct way to do things. She taught us how to behave properly.

We wrote "thank you" notes, and she expected us to get dressed up for Sunday dinner. She taught us that there are rules, customs, and expectations that you should follow. Her lessons have held all of us in good stead.

I have taken after my mom in this regard with my children. I'll say, "Okay, you've had a nice party and gotten your birthday presents. Now it's time to sit down and write 'thank you' notes."

My mom also had a wacky sense of humor that I have inherited. When I was very young, she would pretend that she spoke many foreign languages. She'd speak to me and my friends with these made-up words that maybe hinted at Italian or French or Spanish. She also told my friends that she was an opera singer. She had an eccentric side.

She was also coming out with little quips all the time. If you hit your hand on something or stubbed your toe, Mom would say, "Oh, do it again! I didn't feel it!"

Mom was what the kids today would call spicy. She had that vim and vinegar. Respect for others was never forgotten, but she liked to kid around and could be quite blunt. I can be that way, too, dishing out quips and zingers. I got that from her.

After Deborah and I were engaged, Deborah said to my mom, "Oh, Mom, I really love you." My mother said, "Well, I don't know you well enough to say I love you, but I like you a lot." That is straight talk! It's a bit of a sore subject still, but they did love each other, and Deborah mourned her passing as much as my siblings and I did.

If I was speaking to my mom and starting in with my remark, she would interrupt and break into a song that reflected some of the words I had said. It sort of drove me crazy. Deborah once asked me, "Do you know that you do the exact same thing?" And I do!

I also inherited a sense of style from my mom—both my parents actually. They were very stylish. We went to church socials in Queens on Friday or Saturday nights, and my parents got dressed to the nines. And when we would travel, especially if we took a plane, they were all dolled up. The same is true for me today, and I'm proud to say my son, Nick, is also someone who values looking nice when he ventures out into the world.

On the other hand, my parents were not what you would call "fancy." Dad drove a bus, and Mom was either a stay-at-home mom or a nurse's assistant. But they had a sense of British behavior or codes that they got from their backgrounds, my mother having Jamaican heritage and my father, Bahamian.

I used to love sitting in the kitchen with her. I have fond memories of doing homework at the kitchen table while she was cooking dinner. Or walking into the house and smelling dinner being prepared, which is what made our house a home. I was always happy to be welcomed home by Mom's cooking.

I never cooked with her because our kitchen was tiny and there was a "too-many-cooks" feeling if you know what I mean. With my struggles with weight over the years, it's clear I love to eat, and I like to experiment in the kitchen. So, it just made sense to learn how to cook. I started to cook for myself in college, and she influenced me, obviously.

My mom was also a voracious reader. Her favorite genre was mysteries and thrillers, but she read everything. And she was a devoted reader. I remember my dad coming home from work and being slightly annoyed that Mom hadn't started dinner because she was engrossed by a book. I know that's a tad sexist on his part, but it shows how much she loved to read.

One of the reasons I started writing was to impress my mom. The TV thing was nice, and she appreciated it. But writing a book really meant something to her. She was proud of all her kids and never withheld praise, but the idea that you could write a book was a big deal.

There's a lot of my mother in my parenting. There are rules and expectations. But I also think that my generation has a bit more of a laissez-faire attitude than my parents' generation. You are not going to allow them to do anything that could result in physical or emotional harm. Still, we are not holding the leash as tightly. Of course, I talk a good game and I'm probably tougher than most, but I am not as tough a parent as my mom was.

I never found any of their rules to be unfair or anything like that. My dad used to say, "I'm your father, not your friend." Mom felt the same way. He was Dad, she was

Mom, and I was the kid. I understood it. The expectations were in place, and I did my best to meet them. That's the way it was. I'm a rule follower. I don't know if that came naturally, or if they instilled it in me.

Of course, we were allowed to make mistakes and learn from them. That's so important. There wasn't a stressful environment that demanded constant perfection. There was a demand to do your best and keep trying hard. But that's as it should be, and I have tried to carry that on in my approach to parenting.

My mother was a protective lioness. She loved her family fiercely. I'm the oldest of six—three biological and three adopted. She loved us all equally. Woe betide anyone who dismissed or denigrated one of her children. Long before it was particularly fashionable, she was a strident advocate for her children.

We went to St. Catherine of Siena School in Queens, and my mother volunteered there. But if she thought any teacher wasn't doing what they were supposed to do, she didn't hesitate to speak up.

As a student, I was pretty good in English and history and struggled a bit with math. One day, my social studies teacher mentioned that I was currently failing her class. Well, my mother knew that there was no way on God's green earth that was true. She went to school and made the nun open up and examine her grade book, and, sure enough, she had transposed my grades with somebody else's.

She came home and told me that story. And she also said that I could be doing better in that class! But I was not failing it.

That story sums up my mother's confidence in me. Over time, she was able to instill that in me, because I didn't have it naturally. She believed in me, and I came to believe in myself.

Photo Credit: Christy Turlington

MODELING MOTHERHOOD

Christy Turlington

My mother immigrated to Los Angeles from El Salvador when she was eight years old.

Her father, Horacio, had come before the rest of the family to get settled, and then she and her younger brother, Jaime, followed with their mother, my grandmother, Maria.

My mom's full name is Maria Elizabeth Infante Parker, but she never went by Maria. Her name is Elizabeth, named after the queen of England. She tells us that she learned to speak English reading signs and watching television—she would become a spelling bee champion just a few years after arriving to the US. She would attend community college for a couple of years after graduating from high school before deciding she had places to go, literally, and applying to a stewardess training program for Pan American Airways. Elizabeth Parker, or "Liz" as she has since come to be known by her American friends, started her career with the airline in 1961, and over the next five years, traveled around the world several times, making lifelong friends everywhere she went.

My parents met on a flight from San Francisco to Honolulu on April 12,1965. My dad was on a business trip at the time, and my mom was working the flight. They met and evidently hit it off. My mom was living in Sausalito at the time, and my dad had grown up in a small town in Northern California and had settled in the Bay Area. It turned out my dad was also a pilot, though a recreational one. He was adventurous and intrigued by my mom and all she represented. She was "worldly," as they used to say; independent; and well-traveled, for a young woman in those days. They were married a few years later in San Francisco and headed out to the East Bay area to start their family.

In those days, stewardesses were not permitted to continue flying once they got pregnant. There were many other rules they had to adhere to that involved their appearance, too, which included maintaining their hiring weight. So, after one emergency landing while pregnant with my older sister in Tenerife, the largest of Spain's Canary Islands, my mom left the workforce and transitioned into her next life-changing role: motherhood.

At some point during their courtship, my dad followed Mom's lead and applied for a position with Pan Am, with whom he worked for the duration of his career and the airline's eventual demise many years later. As Dad's career advanced and he was logging the miles to eventually earn his captain's stripes, my mom and my sisters and I became a unit of our own. My dad was away a lot during these early childhood years, and in between trips he would be catching up on sleep or studying his massive training manuals. My grandmother would come up from LA and stay for extended periods of time to help Mom out with us and keep her company while we all enjoyed being the carefree American kids of the 1970s that we were.

By the late '70s, my dad got an exciting job opportunity to move the family to Miami, Florida, and become training captain for the Boeing 747 aircraft. We were all excited about the idea of change but hadn't fully factored in that we would be on the opposite side of the country and thousands of miles from friends and family. Our four years living in Miami were exciting and eye-opening ones. I got my first taste of the American South, with segregation still very much alive and in practice at the time.

When we arrived, we were exposed to cases of police brutality against Blacks and an influx of asylum seekers from Cuba and Haiti who were not welcomed with open arms. My mom's birth country was also at war, just over a thousand miles away by plane. The idea of war was scary to me at that age, and still is. My dad wasn't drafted so never served. The war in El Salvador felt closer to home than the Vietnam War, though it was just as confusing. My mom was concerned about family members who were displaced during this time and was conflicted about the political leanings of her loved ones but also, as a US citizen, disconnected from the parties involved.

Entering adolescence is a challenging time for most and probably not an ideal time for big changes. The chaos around us seemed to mirror what was going on inside me. This is the time when children begin to individuate from their mothers. I was no different. I started to develop my new identity in this new place, just like my mother had done herself more than thirty years before me. Meanwhile, my mom seemed to be thriving being back in a more diverse community and proximity to the rest of the world. No doubt it was her comfort and ease that provided stability for the rest of the family in these otherwise turbulent times. And, as we got older, she started to travel again. She was enjoying the freedom and independence that we were giving back to her.

Our time in Miami came to an abrupt halt when my dad had a heart attack at age fifty. My mom was forty-four when she came to our middle school that day to tell us what had happened and to bring us home before we were able to visit him in the hospital. My dad would be one of the early angioplasty surgery patients, and we would return to California when Pan Am put him on medical leave for an undetermined period of time.

But before leaving Florida, I would get "discovered" as a model while riding my horse after school one day and invited to come to Paris and New York the following summer. My mom was thrilled to have an excuse to travel again as my chaperone, and I was equally thrilled to have her to myself for what seemed like the first time since I was born. We would stroll arm in arm around Paris with my *Plan de Paris* in hand as we explored each arrondissement on foot or via the Metro. Seeing Mom so confident out in the world speaking decent conversational French and navigating the city for us was impressive and gave me a glimpse of who she'd been before us. All those photos she kept of her adventures around the world had stories behind them, and now I was interested in hearing them.

Eventually, I wouldn't need my mom around or want her in the same way. I would spend entire summers in New York until I finally moved there after I turned eighteen but before I graduated from high school. My sisters kept her busy and with plenty to worry about back home while I traveled around the world. Mom and I would write to each other and connect over the phone to share all my adventures during those years, with her wanting to know what I wore, whom I had met, and more details than I could possibly absorb in the moment. She would circle my misspellings and save those letters to point out my poor penmanship when I would come home to visit.

Once I moved to New York City at eighteen and had claimed independence, my definition of adulthood, it was tough to get this little genie back in the bottle. But Mom would not give up on me and encouraged me (begged actually) to graduate. Eventually, I came to my senses and received my high school diploma about a year later, which I sent her in the mail with a note to say, "Here you go, you finally got what you wanted!" I didn't understand how important this choice would be for me at the time, but my mom did.

A few years later, when all three siblings were grown and out of the house, our mom decided to go back to school herself. She went back full-time to pursue a liberal arts degree and graduated at age fifty-three. We were all so proud of her. Not just for the hard work put in to earn the degree, especially so many years after leaving college, but because she had done it for herself. In so doing, she taught me that we are worth the investment in and of ourselves. Two years later, I followed in her footsteps. I applied to NYU to pursue my undergraduate degree.

My mom has taught me through her actions and the lessons learned through the choices she has made throughout her life. Each one of them planted a seed in me and gave me so many options and possibilities to explore for myself. Her ability to stay open and her willingness to share reflections and insights will be what I hold and carry forward. On the shoulders of our mothers, we stand.

Photo Credit: Diane von Furstenberg

LIFE IS LIKE A VICTORY

Diane von Furstenberg

My mother survived because she refused to die. Eighteen months before I was born, my mother was in Auschwitz. Liliane was twenty-two years old and captured by the Nazis for taking part in the Resistance. She worked in the death camp for fourteen months. She did the death march. By the time she was liberated, she weighed just forty-nine pounds, which is very, very little. But she did survive, and she went back home to Belgium. Her parents couldn't believe she came back. Her mother fed her little girl, and within a few months, she had gained back her weight. Her fiancé, who had gone to Switzerland, came back, and they got married. However, her doctor told her that she would have to wait at least three years before she could have a child because otherwise neither she nor her child would survive the pregnancy and birth. Well, sure enough, I was born nine months later. The moment I was born, it was like a victory, and the moment I was born I had already won. Anything that came after that was a plus for us both.

It's with that kind of spirit that I was educated, and therefore I was not allowed to be afraid. If I was afraid of the dark, my mother would lock me in the closet. Of course, today she would go to jail for that! But as a result, I lost my fear of the dark. She never allowed me to blame, or to complain, or anything like that. And that is really the essence of the person that I became.

I have a little note from her. She said, "God saved me, so that I could give you life. You gave me my life back and you are my torch of freedom." She put in my hand the torch of freedom! She equipped me with all of that. I have asked myself, "What is the one thing that defines who I am?" My answer? "It is life. It is the victory of life." If you think like that, then everything else is about gratitude.

For me, gratitude is a gift. Gratitude is seeing the sun go up or sleeping in clean sheets. One thing my mother used to always tell me was that she blessed whoever invented the bed and whoever invented the sheets—because for fourteen months she was sleeping with rats. When you consider whoever invented the bed and the sheets, you have much more of a sense of gratitude. Now every night when I go when to sleep, I really appreciate my sheets.

There are two kinds of people who survived the camps. The ones who didn't die and complain all the time and are sad, and the ones who chose the light and just want to celebrate life.

I will tell you a story. My brother, who is six years younger, had a new office, and he needed a new carpet. He saw this beautiful white carpet, but it was really expensive, and it was all handmade. He debated, "Do I get it or not?" Finally, my mother told him to get it. So, he gets it and enjoys it. Within a week, though, a man came in and was smoking a big, thick cigar and the ash of the cigar falls to the floor and makes a huge hole in this new, white carpet. My brother was devastated, and he called my mother and said that he now had a hole in the beautiful new carpet. Without even thinking, my mother told him that everything that was bad was going to disappear down into that hole. No matter what happened in our lives my mother would find something positive.

My mother didn't want me to carry the sadness of her experience in the camp. She would tell me anecdotes. She would never, ever linger on the suffering. You can't do that with children. She made it almost sound like boarding school. What she was saying was that when you are in a circumstance like that, you can't afford to spend time on the suffering; you have to spend time on the living. She had energy. She was exciting. She was fun. She was all of that. But when she was alone, she had demons, and that fight continued until the very end.

My mother was always strict, but she always pushed me ahead. She never, ever said, "Be careful." No matter what I wanted to do, she just said, "Do it. Go. Go." She wanted me to be in the best position, to have freedom and independence. Now I tell my grandchildren, "The only thing you will regret in your life are the things you don't do or go for." It's so true, isn't it?

Photo Credit: Darren Walker

UNCONDITIONAL LOVE

Darren Walker

Like a lot of women, my mother, Beulah David Spencer, is both a woman of grit and strong character—and, unfortunately, a victim. She grew up in Rayne, Louisiana—the "frog capital of the world"—under very poor circumstances. She was a light-skinned, beautiful Creole girl, and her father left when she was young. Her mother had a hard life. She remarried and had five children. My mother was the only child from her mother's first marriage, and she experienced a lot of terrible sexual abuse when she was young. She had a very, very challenging childhood. When my mother was thirteen, her mother died, and her aunt Rosie (affectionately known as Big) found out at the funeral about the abuse. Literally, while the family was mourning my grandmother's death, Big told my mother's stepfather that she was taking her home to Houston, Texas. So, my mother actually left Rayne and went to Houston to live from age thirteen through high school. But what I found amazing and almost inexplicable was that my mother moved back to Rayne after she graduated high school. I think she wanted to be closer to her siblings.

I was born in Lafayette Charity Hospital, half an hour from Rayne. I never knew my own father, but my mother had two children with him, my sister, Renee, and me. I'm a year and a half older.

Perhaps the biggest gift of the many that my mother gave me came very early in my life, when Beulah resolved to leave Rayne for good. It was a small town, and a very poor, segregated, and racist community. She was rightly worried about the well-being of her children growing up with limited opportunity. Even then, as a poor single mother, she had dreams for her little boy and girl.

So, she moved us to Ames, Texas—population 500—about a two-hour drive from Houston. We moved into a little shotgun house on a dirt road, near where her aunt Ida lived. On the face of it, the move might not have seemed to increase our odds of getting out of poverty. But it proved to be a seminal, life-changing decision on my mother's part. Regrettably, tragically, almost all her siblings and their children stayed in Rayne, and their lives were markedly different in terms of the levels of poverty, incarceration, and educational achievement. I'm deeply grateful to Beulah for so many things in my life, but that was the first big thing: Taking us away from Rayne and bringing us to Ames was such a game changer. When my mother was working, Aunt Ida would take care of us. Aunt Ida was a beloved and important presence in my childhood. It was like having two mothers, and for the most part I recall our time in Ames with blissful joy.

I was an incredibly curious and rambunctious child, and I talked a lot. I talked so much that my mother would offer me a nickel or a quarter to stop. Sometimes she would make up games to get me to stop. We'd be in a car and I would ask question after question, and she would just become exhausted from it and would say, "You can't talk when we go over the bridge, because the bridge will fall down!"

One day, in the spring of 1965, a lady came to our little porch to tell Beulah about the new Head Start program. My mother couldn't sign that document fast enough. I think a part of it was when the lady said she could drop me off for four hours a day and it was free! With unbridled enthusiasm and the thought of four hours of daily freedom, Beulah said, "I will gladly bring him down that dirt road to the Catholic Church school in Ames," which is where the Head Start program was held. My mother was very supportive, and I was completely unaware that I was part of an ambitious educational experiment—the inaugural class of Head Start in America. I loved Head Start—it truly unlocked my love of words, reading, and knowledge. My mother didn't have much money, but she bought the *World Book Encyclopedia*. Every Friday when she got paid, the salesman would come to our house and bring a different letter of the alphabet, and she would give him two dollars, or whatever it was. And so, within a year, I had the *World Book Encyclopedia*. Sometimes she would tell me to look things up and read to her. It was very clear that she had aspirations for me.

Big worked for a wealthy family in River Oaks, the poshest neighborhood in Houston. The Crains were a prominent

Houston family and very good friends with the George H. W. Bush family. Occasionally, my mother would drop us off for the weekend to stay with Big. While she worked in the house, I would go over to the Crains and do yard work. The Crains gave me and my sister the hand-me-downs from their children, which is when I first discovered beautiful clothes. I mean, wow! My mother knew of a photographer in nearby Liberty who took the photos of the family she worked for. He told her he didn't do work for Blacks but that he would take our portraits if we came in before his shop opened on a Saturday morning. The portraits were a triumph. My sister and I were dressed so elegantly—we looked like we were right out of *Ebony* magazine! I was in the most beautiful tweed suit, and my sister was in an elegant, embroidered velvet dress. Mind you, we lived in a shotgun shack, but Beulah had dreams for us, and these portraits manifested her aspirations. When I worked at the Crains I would pack up the shelter magazines and books they discarded in brown paper bags from the Piggly Wiggly supermarket. I would pore over those magazines and books dreaming of a world far beyond Ames, Texas.

I knew that I was gay when I was in elementary school, and my mother knew it too. But she never said, "I know you're a gay little boy." No, what she always said to me was, "You are special. You are going to be successful. You are smart." I never explicitly talked to my mother about being gay until I was an adult living in New York, and I met my partner, David. When I told her she had to meet him, she said, "Well, son, he sounds wonderful! If he makes you happy, your mother is happy. I can't wait to meet him!" And, of course, there began a love affair between the two of them. I think for twenty-five years my mother spoke to David more frequently than she spoke to me.

Aunt Ida also absolutely knew that I was gay. I would help her in the kitchen, and I would help her hang clothes on the line to dry. She had an old-fashioned crank washing tub. I would get the dirty clothes, put them in the tub, and we would work together. All the time, we would talk. She only had a primary school education. She was barely literate, but she would always say, "Baby, you are so sweet," or "Baby, you are such a pretty boy," or "You know, you are so smart with numbers." We would just banter like that. And then some days we would be in the kitchen, and she might cook one of her fabulous coconut vanilla or butter cakes. This was before there was an electric blender, and she'd beat the batter by hand. Then she'd say, "Okay, I'm going to leave some in the bowl just for you." And I would spoon out what she left and think, "Oh, I love this." She was just this amazing lady full of wisdom—not credentialed wisdom but lived experience and a deep faith. She recited verses from Matthew, Peter, and John. She was very devout, and she was just incredibly loving.

And she would laugh at me. She lived in this little railroad shack too. One day we were in the house, and she said to me, "Oh, baby, open the door. I gettin' my hot flashes. It's hot in here." And I said, "Oh, hang on, Auntie, I'll open the doors." Because it was a shotgun house, you opened the front door and the back door, and that's how the air circulated through. Well, at some point soon after that, we were at a relative's house, and it was winter, and they had an open fire because they had no heating. It was really cold outside, and we came inside. My cousin said, "You should get over here by fire so you can get warmed up." And I said, without irony, "Oh, no. I don't want to go by the fire. I'll get hot flashes!"

My mother could not say to me, "You should go to this college because this college is better than that college," or "You should take this course," or "You should major in this," or anything like that. We didn't have those conversations, but she would say, "You are going to go to college, and I just want you to have a better life." She counseled us to stay away from bad people and bad kids. She would say, "If you sleep with dogs, you'll get fleas." But it wasn't that she was a font of inspiring, pithy, witty, literary phrases or advice. It was just the day-in and day-out validation and pragmatic reinforcement that I felt from her. It's very interesting because I know so many gay people in New York who grew up with great privilege and all that money could buy, but they were so tortured about being gay, being different. It was just a completely different thing for them than it was for me. At the time, the American Psychiatric Association defined homosexuality as a psychological disorder. But I never felt like I was a deviant or degenerate. My mother only told me that I was a special and unique child. I feel so sorry for people who grew up being ridiculed, ostracized, and tortured for being gay. For me, there was no torture. Beulah just gave me unconditional love.

Photo Credit: Clarissa Ward

ANNA KARENINA WAS A SLUT

Clarissa Ward

My parents, Donna and Rodney, had a rather eccentric marriage. They separated when I was two and openly had other partners for many years but were still great friends, and Christmases and summers were always spent together as a family. Then, when I was around fifteen, they got back together. They can still drive each other nuts and all, but they live in the British countryside together. Today, they're the epitome of a very dependent, loving couple. I know it works for them.

I came along in January 1980. My parents were living in London at the time. My mother struggled with a baby in the very beginning. She was consumed by her soaring career as an interior designer creating beautiful homes around the world. Obsessive, distracted, and constantly stressed, she was also likely dealing with undiagnosed postpartum depression.

My father was an investment banker workaholic and was not around much either. He went to a British boarding school when he was seven years old and saw his parents once a year. He is incredibly loving and supportive but has a slightly different understanding of how parenting works.

So, yes, I'm an only child!

My mother was very liberal in a lot of ways, but there were things that mattered to her, and she spoke up to me about them. She wanted me to be able to navigate any room and to never feel intimidated or like I didn't belong there.

She has always believed in me and pushed me to push myself and to have high standards for all aspects of my life. She encouraged me to be confident and to strive for excellence and not be complacent. While she was pretty liberal in her rules and I could do almost anything I wanted, there was a baseline of expected academic excellence, and falling below that wasn't to be tolerated.

Along with this liberal approach and high expectations in certain areas, my mother could also be very blunt. We were on vacation when I was fourteen, and I was reading *Anna Karenina*. I was so devastated when I got to the end; Anna had obviously committed suicide, and I was sobbing. My mother was having a cocktail and said to me, "Oh, toughen up, Clarissa, please. Anna was a slut."

That's kind of my mom in a nutshell.

She was very direct and pulled no punches. In retrospect, it was enormously helpful to me as a journalist.

Growing up, my mother really did not excel when I was sad. But now I'm old and wise enough to understand why. Mom's reaction would always be to try to make it better. She wanted to control everything as much as possible. She wanted everyone to be happy and everything to be perfect. That was tricky for me, because when I was feeling really sad about experiences I'd had, I didn't really know how to slow down, take a breath, and let myself feel sad for a little bit.

Her attitude was how she dealt with all the challenges of her childhood. That's what she had to do to get along and survive. Her mother had bipolar disorder. and, as a result, my mom had a really difficult childhood. So, when she went to boarding school in California, she was very happy for the first time. It was like an escape for her.

When she was younger and having a difficult time with her mother, she used to sit, close her eyes, and say, "I'm going to be a beautiful, international, wealthy career woman. I'm going to travel the world, and I'm going to marry a brilliant man who loves me."

She was just fixated on it, and she made it happen. I think she passed that on to me. This idea of not accepting anything less than the best, and, whatever you put your mind to, you can do. You can will the future for yourself if you work at it hard enough.

She's made me a stronger person in a world where a lot of people coddle their children. I probably coddle mine. My mother was not a coddler. She was loving and built this life for me, so I could be the best version of myself that I could be—but, along the way, she was also very tough.

Yet, my mother was very good at intimacy, closeness. You could tell her anything. She was always taking me to do cool stuff, and we would sit up in bed and eat sushi and talk about her boyfriends. We had a close friendship, but it was a less traditional version of mother and daughter. But it's who she is. She has the same thing with my children. There is no awkwardness with my mom.

My boys are eight, five, and two. I think I will have a similar relationship in the sense that I want my kids to be able to talk to me about anything, and I don't want them to be doing stuff behind my back. I'd rather know about it and be able to exert some influence that way.

And my mother was very much like that. I would tell her if I drank alcohol, smoked cigarettes, or had a boyfriend. I would tell her all that stuff, and she might not always approve, but I never felt like I needed to hide things from her. And, frankly, as long as I got good grades, everything else was "Okay, that's great."

When it came to those grades, she was, again, very straightforward. She said to me, "You can go to Oxford or Cambridge, or Harvard or Yale, but *you* choose." She was telling me in her own way not to accept "no" for an answer. You tell yourself you're going to a great college, and you figure out how to make it happen.

With another kid, that approach might have been a disaster. But with me, it gave me the focus and rigor that I needed, because my default position might have been to accept less.

My mother just never let up on pushing me to high standards. I started out as a producer in TV, and I enjoyed it. I didn't need to be in front of the camera. My mother saw it differently.

She told me, "You're a very verbal person. You connect with people. This is what you were born to do. I can see it. You should be able to see it, and you shouldn't run away from it because it scares you a little."

My professional success is in large part due to her. She's my toughest critic, but she is also my fiercest advocate. She watches every live shot I do. She will send me a message that I need a little more concealer under my left eye. To this day, she'll tell me, "I don't like that shirt on you."

One time my mom came to visit me at college. I told her that there was this guy I liked, who was my very good friend as well. We ended up smoking grass with my friends, which again shows that my mother is not like your ordinary mom.

At one point, there was silence in the conversation, and my mother said to a gathering of me and my friends, "Do you know Clarissa refuses to see a gynecologist?"

And it wasn't even true! My friends were crying with laughter and telling me my mom was the funniest person they'd ever met. And I was thinking she would be a lot funnier to me if she was someone else's mom.

It all fell into place for me when I started having children and became a mom myself. My eldest son has what is called a de novo mutation, a random act of nature in which a gene mutation appears. He is a very sweet little boy, but he doesn't speak, and he will almost certainly always live with us and not out on his own.

Yet, my mother, who spent her career trying to make things perfect and beautiful, loves my eldest son intensely and with a deep and absolute appreciation of all that he is.

It is very moving to see them together. In her own way, my mother has an enormous heart, and even though my son is different, she is able to love him unconditionally.

She loves him in all of his unique ways of interacting with people. He goes into her room at 6:00 a.m., while she's fast asleep, and climbs into bed with her. He steals her iPad. She can't get enough of him, and he adores her.

My mother always struggled to be gentle because she had to be so tough growing up. But she's also loving and sensitive. And with my son, you see that, actually, she is not tough at all.

My mother has given me a wonderful piece of advice about being a mother. One time I was lamenting that my job takes me away from my boys so often and that I am regularly quite busy when I am home. I asked her, "How present am I as a mother? Am I doing enough for them?"

"First of all, you're an amazing mother," said my mom. "So, forget about those questions and doubts. The only thing that matters is that your children feel deeply loved, secure, stable, and like they have a happy home they thrive in. Everything else is organization."

I think that is so true and has helped me so much. My guilt is really an expression of my sadness when I miss something of theirs. But I have organized our household in such a way, with my parents close by, that it is all pretty smooth. My kids have a great life, and they can handle it if I go away for two weeks, because they know I'll come back.

They know I love them, and they are secure in the routine of their lives. It's much harder on me than it is on them.

I'm so grateful my mother instilled that in me. Give them love and stability, and the rest is logistics.

Photo Credit: Ali Wentworth

NOBODY GOES TO THE BAHAMAS
IN JULY

Ali Wentworth

My mother, Mabel Hobart Wentworth Brandon Cabot—but universally known as Muffie—is from an old New England family. Of course, "Muffie" is a quintessential preppy, stuffy sort of nickname. It turned out to suit her perfectly though. She's very reserved and a bit puritanical but also inclined to dig in during tough times and pull herself up by the bootstraps, as the saying goes.

Her birth name is Mabel, but her family used to tease her about it with a little song:

> *Mabel, Mabel strong and able*
> *Get your elbows off the table*
> *This is not a horse's stable*
> *But the children's dining table*

She didn't like the teasing, and when somebody started calling her "Muffie," she just adopted that as her name. She certainly kept the "strong and able" part though.

My mother was shaped most and became the woman she is by the time and events of the mid-1960s. During roughly a single year, my mother got divorced from my father, and both of her parents and her only sister died. Today, I can't personally imagine that, and I think that some women might have fallen, understandably, into a severe depression. But my mother reached for those afore-mentioned bootstraps and pulled herself up into a great life that taught me a lot. It was sink or swim for her, and she is still swimming today. I believe that those times, and her reaction to them, empowered her and brought out the lion-ess in her. She certainly became a role model for me.

At that time, she was a single mother of three and doing a lot of campaigning for the Kennedys, though for a while she was still on the fringe of Washington, DC, politics. After about six years of single motherhood, she married Henry Brandon, who was the Washington correspondent for *The Sunday Times* of London. She was not on the fringe of DC society anymore. She suddenly found herself in the center of it and needing to attend and throw lavish dinner parties because Henry needed to make connections and establish a standing in Washington society and politics. His job was defined by his access to the newsmakers, and you have to go out and create it.

As a result, Mom was sort of pushed into being this hostess and partygoer and that really wasn't who she was, certainly not when we were young. For several years, my mom had been working a bit, but mostly she was taking care of her children. Now they were having big, fancy par-ties and going to the British embassy all the time. It seemed like every night my mom was in a long dress and going out somewhere.

I was about five when this fairly dramatic shift in our lives happened, and I remember all kinds of well-known people coming in and out of our house. I came to believe that we shared her with her job, and this started around this time. My mother became this formidable person—and still is a force to be reckoned with—and it started in those early days of her marriage to Henry. There was a cover story about her in *Washingtonian* magazine that called her the most feared woman in DC. She is much more complicated than that and is in fact a rather layered person, comfortable in a variety of situations, which I greatly admire.

I saw that, in part, she was successful because she could connect with everybody. She could be laughing hysterically with Luciano Pavarotti at a party and then be joking around or telling a dirty joke to a lobsterman when we were on a vacation in Maine. I have always respected that aspect of my mother, the way she treated everybody the same. She was never a snob. She was just as kind to the guy that pruned our hedges as she was to Mikhail Gorbachev's wife. To her, human beings are human beings, and that is a valuable lesson she taught me.

It is amazing to watch my mother in a room full of people. She is mesmerizing in her ability to bring people together and introduce them and open up people's worlds. She does this dance of "Oh, Charlie, meet Lisa. She has this amazing sculpture that you would love." She is truly remarkable in this way, and she would never let anybody sit alone in a corner.

Despite her earlier Democratic Party affiliation, eventually, she became the social secretary for First Lady Nancy Reagan and was helping to put on state dinners for the likes of the queen of England. I'm sure she was no pushover when deciding who got to socialize with the Reagans. Yet, she was also at our house on the weekends in her blue jeans, working in the garden, and yelling at us to clean our rooms.

When we were growing up, Mom definitely had two sides to her. She was this glamorous woman with a helmet of hair-sprayed hair in an Armani gown trying to figure out table seatings that wouldn't start a nuclear war. And she was also this very down-to-earth mother that you could talk to about anything. She had a very full life, and I saw that she didn't relegate herself to being a stay-at-home mom, not that there's anything wrong with that choice. She wanted to experience the world and meet interesting people. She took me to Europe when she was doing underwriting for an arts project for the Ford Motor Company. We held Renoirs in our hands. She introduced me to writers and artists all the time.

Once, I had a meeting with Goldie Hawn. For her movie *Protocol*, Goldie shadowed my mother at the White House for a couple of days. She told me, "No matter where we went, everyone knew your mom!"

It was the same up in Maine, where she had a house for many years. The local seamstress told me that she used to do a regular "stitch and bitch" with my mom as they went over town gossip and news.

I loved that world citizen aspect of her life, the idea of seizing every opportunity to see the world and know people. I love that down-to-earth and relatable quality she has. I found it incredibly compelling and definitely instilled it in myself. And, as a mother now myself, I try to instill it in my children.

As a daughter, I felt she was a great role model because she could be both of those people: a high-powered and respected professional and an attentive mother. She kept it up, too, when she had my younger sister and became a mother of four.

I learned from my mom that women can't have it all, but we can sometimes figure out how to do both. I watched her do both her roles and applied it to my own life and career when I became a mother. When my two girls were young, I realized that, instead of acting, I could write books when they were at school, and I'd be there when they came home, which is the way my husband, George Stephanopoulos, and I wanted to raise them. I found that it is possible to have a meaningful job and be a thoughtful, present mom.

Now, part of who I am is that I reacted to her more reserved, genteel ways. As the saying goes, my mother never peed in the shower. I rebelled against that sort of formality and primness. But it has made for some amusing moments for sure.

About twenty-five years ago, I was living in Los Angeles and had been engaged to someone for eight years. I finally ended the engagement because I realized I didn't want to marry him. I think my mother was relieved that I broke up with him.

I assumed that he would be incredibly depressed that I had left him and that his heart would be broken. I was sure that he would be face down for months, if not years.

But a few weeks later, when I called our old answering machine to check on something, I heard a message that said, "I am calling to confirm the private charter for you and your wife to the Bahamas."

I was completely taken aback. I couldn't believe he had moved on so quickly and that he had arranged a private charter. He never took me anywhere in a chartered plane. I was absolutely devastated.

This happened just before the Fourth of July, and I skipped the party I was supposed to go to. I stayed in my Land's End nightgown crying and thinking I had made this horrible mistake and had destroyed my life.

After three days of not eating or showering, I called my mother and told her the story. Then there was a long pause.

Finally, my mother said, "Oh, Ali, nobody goes to the Bahamas in July."

It was such a "Muffie" thing to say, and it actually pulled me out of it. My mother's position was why would you even want to be with a man who would take you to the Bahamas in July? She was absolutely serious, and it made me laugh and I thought, *Well, in a way, she's right.*

My mother's patrician personality also showed up in how she expressed herself. She did use the old, reliable New

England phrase about bootstraps. She also says, "Keep the wolf at the door." She means that you should be modest regarding money, have enough to live on, but don't be boastful or flashy about it. She'd prefer no discussion of money, actually.

She wasn't frugal, but she believed that you have to be careful with money and that it all could be taken away at any moment. You only need what you need. She still says to me, "Be careful with your money."

I'll tell her, "Mom, we're okay. We're fine." I could say to her, "We have a hundred billion dollars in the bank." And she'd say, "Well, you do *now*."

If she were Jeff Bezos's mother, she'd say, "Do you really need such a *big* boat?"

My mother also has a stock response to bad moments or events. I was attacked and robbed by some gang members in Los Angeles. I was beaten up a little, and the guy I was with was stabbed. I called my mom and told her what happened. She said, "Go check yourself into the Four Seasons."

I went, though I don't really know why, and then the phrase and idea became a recurring thing with us. The day of the 9/11 attack, when I was living in New York City, my mother was the only one to get through on my cell phone. She said, "Go check into the Four Seasons." George and I went, and when he asked me why, I said, "It's just what we do." I guess my mother thinks it's better to see the world end with room service.

My mother was also a terrible disciplinarian. If we got in trouble for being sassy or missing curfew, she would say,

"You're in trouble. Go to your room. No dinner for you." But ten minutes later, she'd knock on your door with a tray holding a better dinner than everyone else just had, including a fabulous dessert. I have fully inherited this quality. I cannot get mad at my children, and I cannot discipline them. It hurts me much more than it hurts them.

Now I like to watch her with my children. She schools them a little bit, as in "We don't talk that way," or "We don't do that." She's big on manners and decorum. She still believes in handwritten thank you notes. I make my girls do it, but they don't have any friends who do. They text emojis.

She also used to have them get in bed with her and read to them. I don't remember her doing that for me, but it's sweet to see.

I love that my mother also likes to pass on family history. She'll tell my daughters, "You know your great-grandmother made a boat out of yak skin and sailed across the Yellow River." She loves the cultural idea of passing on stories. And my daughters hear family stories from me too. Like how nobody goes to the Bahamas in July.

Photo Credit: Susan Wojcicki

THINK FOR YOURSELF

Susan Wojcicki

My mother, Esther, learned from an early age to think for herself. She came from a very traditional family where she was told that her life plan should just be to get married and have children. She's the daughter of Jewish-Russian religious refugees from Siberia and Ukraine. My grandparents arrived in the US separately, met each other in New York City, and got married. Neither of my grandparents had much of an education, so they were limited in their ability to earn a living. My grandfather was a struggling artist who made an income doing tombstone art, and my mother worked as a salesclerk. They were always struggling financially. After my mother was born, they moved to Southern California. She was the valedictorian of her high school class and became the first person in her family to go to college, graduating from UC Berkeley. Her parents would ask her, "Why do you even want to go to college?" She realized she needed an education to have more opportunities.

I grew up in Palo Alto, California, where my mom became a high school teacher, which was one of the few career options open to her. My dad was a professor of physics at Stanford. When I was little, I heard stories about the suffering that my mom's parents went through during the pogroms in Eastern Europe. My grandparents told me about people being beaten and dying and being worried for their lives. At a young age, I realized how much I had access to that my grandparents did not have, including an education. I had a peaceful and happy childhood, but I also understood that life can be very hard, and it took a lot of work and sacrifice to enable me to be where I was. I knew I came from a family that had faced a lot of challenges, and I was very fortunate to have the opportunity to grow up where I did.

Before she was even a teenager, my mother had two incredibly traumatic experiences. She had a much younger brother who overdosed on aspirin at two years old. These many years later, it's still an emotional topic in our family. Her parents didn't have access to medical insurance or good medical advice, and he died, although he could have been saved with the right medical attention. Seeing her brother die and realizing her parents were unable to prevent it left an impression on her. Then, she had a second experience where her family had carbon monoxide in their home, but her parents didn't understand the danger. They told her to go lie down, but she knew the danger and she went outside to get help. She said to herself, "I'm from an immigrant family. My parents aren't educated. They can't make all the right decisions for me, and if I don't think for myself, then I could die too." These experiences never left her. Early on, she began to question people in authority and not simply trust the accepted wisdom.

When I was a kid, this aspect of her personality was sometimes very embarrassing to me. I'm the oldest of three girls, and we would always have stories about my mom and the unusual things that she would ask or do. One of my earliest memories is being pushed along in a stroller while my mom went door to door, handing out fliers to protest a property development on the Stanford campus. My dad traveled a lot, and my mother was the one who fixed things around the house. She even took an automotive class so she could fix the car without having to rely on the mechanic. We had an upstairs bathroom that once had a clogged toilet, and she didn't want to call the plumber. We helped her get the outdoor hose up to the second floor, put it down the pipe, and then turned it on to flush out whatever was in the toilet. I don't know if that's a good plumbing technique or not, but it was a very interesting way of just fixing the problem yourself! She was all about self-reliance.

Thinking unconventionally was also a hallmark of hers, and she never hesitated to question the experts. She would challenge them, never afraid to try to understand better what was *really* happening. When you're a child, this kind of behavior by your mother can be embarrassing. I think she was probably seen as a difficult parent, certainly by our doctors—but we got pretty good medical care!

In many ways, this behavior also inoculated me against my own feelings of embarrassment, which has been very valuable. I was already embarrassed all the time as a kid, so nobody can really say or do anything that would make me embarrassed today. I might acknowledge mistakes, issues, and concerns, but I'm not afraid of being embarrassed, making mistakes, or asking hard questions.

By the time I was in high school, I was already in the process of evolving my own thinking about challenging authority. My mom was an English teacher at the same high school, and she was arguing with the school about the changes they were planning to the English curriculum. She led a group of parents to also raise issues with my teacher, who was the head of the English department. I felt very uncomfortable; it was an awful moment for me. I would tell my mom, "Please don't call my teacher and complain, because the teacher is going to punish me and change my grade." My mom would say, "No, don't worry about it. Your teacher's not going to do anything bad to you."

I thought that when people spoke up and expressed their opinions, there would be negative consequences. But watching her, gradually a light bulb went off. I realized it was really the opposite. When you speak up, people take you more seriously. I had assumed the teachers would punish me because my mom was speaking up, but I learned that they had respect for her and for what she was saying. When you speak up, it can be controversial, but there's also respect that comes along with it. I see this with my own kids. If I ever comment on something, my kids worry about what's going to happen. I tell them, "No, it's actually good if I speak up. People will be more aware and probably be more careful about their future actions. That's a good thing."

My mom always said that if you complain about something that didn't go the right way, you're actually helping other people. If she just let a doctor or restaurant continue doing things the wrong way and didn't challenge them in some way, the next person who comes along will have the same experience.

I can see how this influenced my decisions. My career path was about choosing new industries that were undergoing change, believing that not everyone knew the answers, and having the confidence that a different type of world could exist. It's been about challenging the establishment. At Google and YouTube, we've innovated in ways that people didn't think were possible before.

I would say the number one gift that my mom gave me was the ability to think independently and to not always take the word of experts. She taught me to think for myself and to question what was most important.

I came to appreciate my mother's parenting technique even more when I became a parent myself. I started thinking a lot about what she did and how I could repeat it. What were the good things she did? My mom used a lot of positive encouragement. As both a teacher and a parent, I think she fundamentally believes that you need to understand the psychology of the child and motivate them so that they can motivate themselves. You can't force kids to do anything. You really need to help them *want* to do it. That's something I have passed on to my kids.

As a teenager, I also recognized that my mom didn't have any of the strict rules that a lot of my friends had about using the car or participating in certain activities. My mother was really a way cooler mom, and she just had a more flexible approach to managing me as a teenager.

One of the things that's hard as a parent is when your kids take an interest in something that you know nothing about or that you didn't think should be their interest. That's happened to me with all my kids. Their interests have been different from what I initially expected. But I recognized from my mom that it's okay. The best thing to do is to figure out how to support them and to understand how they're thinking. You have to help them motivate themselves to be successful in what they want to do.

My mom is now in her eighties and has an amazing ability to continue learning. She wrote a book, she's working with young people about ways to reform education, and she became a public speaker. When I was young, she taught me to think for myself. As I grow older, I hope I continue to follow her model and never stop evolving, growing, and learning.

Susan Wojcicki, former YouTube CEO, passed away on August 9, 2024. This tribute to her mother appears posthumously in honor of Susan's remarkable life.

ACKNOWLEDGMENTS

We would like to thank several people, without whom this book would not be possible.

First, Kristin van Ogtrop, our agent who believed in the possibility of this book from the very beginning and helped guide us through the entire process. And then our editor and publisher, Gretchen Young and Regalo Press, whose philosophy is to give back from the proceeds of the sale of their books to help support worthy causes that help to make the world a better place. At Regalo Press, we'd also like to thank Madeline Sturgeon, Caitlin Burdette, Allie Woodlee, and Donna DuVall for all that they did to help bring this book to life.

John Hassan was an invaluable storyteller who helped us structure many of these stories.

Karyn Leibovich on *Sesame Street*'s production team helped secure the contributors whom you read about, and Elizabeth Perez helped us arrange the time for many of us to chat—no easy task!

Finally, there was Amanda Sammartano, whose enthusiasm, project coordination, idea generation, and overall unwavering and sustaining support knew no bounds. We never would have crossed the finish line without her!

Of course, we are indebted to all our colleagues at Sesame Workshop that we have worked with over the years who believe deeply in the Workshop's mission to help children everywhere grow smarter, stronger, and kinder. You inspire us each and every day. Your dedication to the mission drives us to give back all the authors' proceeds to help the Workshop continue to provide access to quality early learning to help put children on a path to thrive.

And to all the mothers, this book reaffirms what we already knew. That your support and the example you set are a bedrock for building a meaningful life.